Start Your Own

HOME INSPECTION SERVICE

Additional titles in *Entrepreneur's* **Startup Series**

Start Your Own

Bar or Club

Bed & Breakfast

Business on eBay

Car Wash

Child Care Service

Cleaning Service

Clothing Store

Coin-Operated Laundry

Consulting

Crafts Business

e-Business

e-Learning Business

Event Planning Business

Executive Recruiting Service

Freight Brokerage Business

Gift Basket Service

Growing and Selling Herbs and Herbal Products

Import/Export Business

Information Consultant Business

Law Practice

Lawn Care or Landscaping Business

Mail Order Business

Medical Claims Billing Service

Office and Administrative Support Service

Online Education Business

Personal Concierge Service

Personal Training Business

Pet-Sitting Business

Restaurant and Five Other Food Businesses

Retail Business and More

Seminar Production Business

Staffing Service

Travel Business

Vending Business

Wedding Consultant Business

Wholesale Distribution Business

Entrepreneur
MAGAZINE'S

start up

2ND EDITION

Start Your Own

HOME INSPECTION SERVICE

Your Step-by-Step Guide to Success

Entrepreneur Press and Cheryl Kimball

Ep
Entrepreneur
Press

Editorial Director: Jere L. Calmes
Managing Editor: Marla Markman
Cover Design: Beth Hansen-Winter
Production and Composition: Eliot House Productions

This publication is designed to provide accurate and authoritative information in regard to the subject matter covered. It is sold with the understanding that the publisher is not engaged in rendering legal, accounting or other professional services. If legal advice or other expert assistance is required, the services of a competent professional person should be sought.

Library of Congress Cataloging-in-Publication Data

Start your own home inspection service/by Entrepreneur Press and Cheryl Kimball.—2nd ed.

    p.   cm.

Includes index.

ISBN-13: 978-1-59918-128-8 (alk. paper)

ISBN-10: 1-59918-128-2 (alk. paper)

    1. Dwellings—Inspection. 2. Small business. I. Kimball, Cheryl. II. Entrepreneur Press. III. Title: Home inspection business.

TH4817.5.S73 2007

643'.12—dc22   2007026696

Printed in Canada

12 11 10 09 08 07   10 9 8 7 6 5 4 3 2 1

Contents

Preface xi

Chapter 1
The Entryway 1
    Home Anatomy 101 2
        Inspection Lesson 3
    Business Ups and Down 4
        About Your Clients 4
    Breaking In 5
    The Right Stuff. 7
        Limber Up 7
        Generally Speaking. 8
        Down to Specifics 9
        Sixth Sense 10

Chapter 2
The Foundation 11
    Survey Says 12
        Market Share. 12
    Franchise or Independent? 15
    Got a Plan? 16
    The Name Game 17

On a Mission 17
On Location 18
Movin' on Up 20

Chapter 3
The Cost Factor **21**
Start-Up Costs 22
Getting Educated 22
Getting Professional Advice 23
Getting Insured 24
Supplying Your Office 24
Getting Equipped 24
Tool Basics 25
Computer Equipment Basics 25
Office Equipment Basics 27
Not on the Critical List 27
Surfing the Net 29
Putting It All Together 29

Chapter 4
A Sound Structure **35**
Licenses/Permits 36
Business Structure 36
Side by Side 37
Your Lawyer 38
Legal Challenges 38
Insurance 40
Get It in Writing 41
Ethics and Standards 43

Chapter 5
Nuts and Bolts **45**
It's Elementary 46
Sherlock Homes 46
Stories from the Trenches 47
Going Along on an Inspection 49
Roofing Revealed 50
Exterior Exam 50
Amped Up 52
Code not Required 53

Leaky Pipes 54
Down the Drain. 54
Attic Static 55
Finishing Touches 56
Potential Problems. 56
Service Above and Beyond 57
Radon Rundown 57
Reporting Your Findings 58
The Checklist Report 58
The Narrative Report 59
Delivery 60
The Follow-Up 60
Pricing Your Services. 61
Collecting Fees 61

Chapter 6
Upgrading Your Expertise 71

Train, Don't Strain. 72
Compare, Compare 72
Live and In Person 73
Home Study. 73
Online Training. 74
Course Pricing. 74
Why Train? 75
Get Professional. 76
Branching Out 77
Expert Witness. 77
Special Investigations. 78
Other Offshoots. 78

Chapter 7
Selling Yourself. 81

Getting the Word Out. 82
Creating a Professional Image 82
Cross-Promotion. 84
Networking 84
Dynamite Direct Mail 85
Direct e-Mail 85
Web Power. 86
The Highlights 86

Images 86
Qualifications. 87
Your Staff 87
Tips 87
Testimonials 87
Links. 87
Products 88
Site Design. 88
Yellow Pages. 88
Special Promotions 88
Hiring a Professional. 89
Customer Service. 90

Chapter 8
Managing Employees and Finances. 91
Income and Operating Expenses. 92
Employee Basics. 93
Employee Payroll/Taxes 94
Answering Options 95
Outsourcing Options. 95
Money Matters. 96
Bookkeeping 96
Record-Keeping. 98
Financial Statements 98
Funding Your Start-Up 99

Chapter 9
Inspection Lessons: Pass or Fail 101
Common Pitfalls 102
It's All About Perspective 102
Experience Necessary 103
Recipe for Success 103
Take the High Road 104
Take It Slowly 104
A Service-Oriented Business. 105

Appendix
Home Inspection Resources 107
Associations 107
Books 108

Conventions and Expos. 108
Experts 108
Forms. 109
Franchises. 109
Government Agencies 109
Home Study/Correspondence Courses 110
Radon Testing 110
Reporting Software 110
Successful Home Inspection Service Owners. 110
Tools. 111
Trade Publications. 111
Training Schools 111

Glossary **113**

Index **115**

Preface

There really isn't a bad time to enter the business of home inspection. You'll be interested to know that some skilled and dedicated inspectors can make well into the three-figure category—emphasis, however, on the words "skilled" and "dedicated." It's these two qualities that will ultimately determine who will rise like cream to the top of this business and who won't.

And that's the focus of this book—to help you learn what you can do to establish a profitable service while cultivating a work ethic of personal excellence. It will be this attention to detail and commitment to quality that will set you apart from the rest of the pack. You will get to explore the nuts-and-bolts descriptions of how to start and run your business and to examine the qualities needed to be a top-notch home inspector with insightful personal anecdotes from the day-to-day lives of successful inspector entrepreneurs. Get ready, and this book will take you on an informative, motivational journey to what will hopefully become a prosperous, satisfying, and long-lasting career.

Happy Inspecting!

1

The
Entryway

Whether the housing boom is in building new homes, purchasing existing homes, or buying foreclosure properties, the wise buyer is making her agreement contingent on a satisfactory home inspection. Not only are home inspection services used by the consumer-conscious buyer, but most lenders require a professional home inspection before they will close a mortgage on a property. Can there be a better type of business to be in than one that is in demand in either an up or down market?

Just what does the home inspection business involve? A home inspector examines the major systems and components of the property—from roof to foundation, from ceiling to floor, from basement to attic. A home inspection helps buyers understand the condition of the property they're interested in purchasing and, hopefully, prevents any unforeseen repair bills down the road.

Homebuyers are not the only parties to request inspections, though. The seller of a home might also request one to get an accurate assessment of the property. This could head off any potential lawsuits stemming from failure to disclose existing problems within the home. And lenders often require a home inspection prior to closing on a mortgage to ensure that the house they are lending money on is worth the amount of the mortgage.

Home Anatomy 101

According to the American Society of Home Inspectors (ASHI), "Home inspections were being performed in the mid-1950s and, by the early 1970s, were considered by many consumers to be essential." Homebuyers wanted to know more about the properties they were considering purchasing. To meet this demand, home inspectors with backgrounds in construction, engineering, architecture, renovation, or municipal building inspection were best suited to the job, according to ASHI.

Part of the growth of the home inspection field, says Keith Morgan of the California Real Estate Inspection Association, has been fueled by the legal community and insurance companies. Home buying is not exempt from the litigousness of modern society.

After several decades of growth, the home inspection industry has now topped $1 billion. According to industry experts, more than 80 percent of homebuyers nationwide request a home be professionally inspected; 2004 figures show an estimated 25,000 home inspectors.

What kind of salaries do home inspectors take home? According to Mallory Anderson, Executive Director of the National Association of Home Inspectors in Minneapolis, a start-up home inspection business could earn between $20,000 and $40,000 the first year, as long as the business is marketed properly. A start-up scenario, Anderson says, would look something like this:

- $3,000 for training
- $2,500 for business equipment (computer, printer, fax, etc.)
- $2,500 for marketing literature

- $10,000 cash reserve/living expenses if you don't have another job
- $3,500 professional liability insurance
- $500 for a business license, depending on the requirements of the state you are operating in.

Anderson's advice in the current "seller's market" is for the professional home inspector to "consistently market and network with other industry professionals. The home inspector will need to market a little harder to keep ahead of

Stat Fact
According to the Federal Trade Commission, nearly half of U.S. homeowners who buy previously owned houses have to make unexpected repairs. Over half the problems requiring repair come up during the first six months of ownership.

the competition in his or her area. The inspector will also need to offer other specialized inspection services such as radon, water, lead, mold, septic, termite, as well as other ancillary services to complement his business."

Inspection Lesson

In many cases, prospective homeowners contact a home inspector once they have signed on the dotted line. In some states, sellers may opt for a pre-listing inspection before putting their home up for sale. The advantage of this approach is that the seller gets information on the condition of the house before the sale, avoiding the input of a potential buyer on how to do the repairs. A pre-sale inspection can also help hasten the sale and generate a higher price.

A professional home inspection should prepare the homebuyer or seller with documented facts about the physical condition of the structure and all its working components. It is up to the inspector to report his findings back to the prospective buyer or seller. A good report should cover such areas as: the exterior and interior, the roof, structure, plumbing, electrical, heating and cooling, insulation, ventilation, lot grading, insects, vermin and decay, landscaping, and environmental and safety issues.

Stat Fact
Every day, homebuyers save thousands of dollars through information provided by their home inspector. A home inspector's keen eye can help nip a small home repair problem in the bud, before it becomes a major one.

While the home inspection industry is still largely unregulated in most states, this is changing. Make sure you check the current regulations in your state (see Chapter 4 for more information on this topic). In addition, professional associations such as ASHI provide some useful guidelines for home inspectors. For example, ASHI has developed a "Standards of Practice" listing everything a home inspector should inspect, as well as everything a home inspector should not be responsible for checking. These standards, along with ASHI's "Code of Ethics," are a resource that home inspectors can consult when deciding what they need to include in their own home inspection process. Visit the ASHI Web site at www.ashi.org for more information on these guidelines.

Business Ups and Down

Stat Fact

According to the *Occupational Outlook Handbook* from the U.S. Dept. of Labor, Bureau of Labor Statistics, the field of home inspection is expected to continue to outpace other occupations through 2014. Visit the Bureau of Labor Statistics' web site at http://stats.bls.gov to view an online version of the *Occupational Outlook Handbook.*

Although there is the predictable rise and fall of the real-estate market, there seems to be no bad time to enter the home inspection field.

According to the article "On the Road to Recovery" in *Realtor* Magazine Online, David Lereah of the National Association of Realtors expects the 2007 slowdown in home sales to turn around fully in many markets by the end of 2008. And the U.S. Department of Housing and Urban Development (HUD) recently reported that national homeownership rate rose to a high of 68.1 percent, dropping a percentage point from 2005. Not a huge drop, and one that is easily recovered. In an interview for *The Real Estate Inspector*, a publication for real-estate professionals, Mike Sterling, chair of the ASHI Standards Committee, says that the home inspection industry has "grown significantly in the last decade." In response to this growth, ASHI revised their "Standards of Practice" in January 2000. The standards, according to Sterling, had not been revised since 1992. In addition to the fact that "inspectors are now more educated and more capable," Sterling cited the sophistication and higher expectations of both homebuyers and real estate agents as reasons for revising the standards.

About Your Clients

As a home inspector, prospective homebuyers and sellers will be your customers, of course. Warranty companies and banks may also be clients (see Chapter 2 for more information). And then there are the realtors . . .

Dealing with realtors is a large part of the home inspection business, and, like it or not, they are a legitimate source of referrals. However, to help define their role in the real-estate transaction, some home inspectors choose to view themselves as consumer advocates or even educators. Keeping such a focus, they say, helps them avoid the appearance of conflict of interest (e.g., giving a more favorable inspection report in order to not sour a real estate agent's deal) and maintain a respectful autonomy in the minds of everyone involved in the home inspection process. But there's no denying that it's to home inspectors' benefit if the realty world is aware of their services. It's also to a realtor's benefit, as home inspections can ward off potential lawsuits resulting from a realtor's failure to disclose existing problems.

Martin H., an actor-turned-home-inspector in Southern and Central California, says he joined the Association of Realtors in his area and showed up every morning at their multiple listings services meetings. "I was able to introduce myself [to] a number of other affiliate members of the association. And slowly but surely, I started to work. I took out ads in the Yellow Pages and distributed fliers through a flier distribution service," he says.

Woody L., a franchisee in Glendale, Arizona, was very curious to hear how real estate folk felt about home inspectors, so he just asked them: "Some thought home inspectors were a pain in the neck. Others thought they were only needed on houses that had been remodeled a lot. But the most successful agents and brokers I spoke to said they could see the day when every deal had an inspection."

Breaking In

Bob Mulloy, formerly a teacher of the business of home inspection at Northeastern University, and editor-in-chief of *The Inspector*, a publication of ASHI's New England chapter, had been a contractor for a number of years before he got into the home inspection business about 18 years ago. His sister-in-law, a real-estate broker at the time, said she was starting to "see these guys called home inspectors" and thought Mulloy would be good at doing what they were doing.

"That one comment," says Mulloy, in East Bridgewater, Massachusetts, "kindled a spark that has become a lifetime quest. I did about one year's worth of research and timidly hung out my shingle as a home inspector. The profession was in its infancy at the time, and we kind of stumbled and learned to walk together."

Stat Fact

According to the U.S. Bureau of Labor Statistics, the majority of home inspectors come to the field from either an engineering or construction trade.

Martin H. discovered home inspection after working in construction for a while. "I was a working actor for a number of years; then things slowed down, and I had a friend who got me into the construction business," he says. Eventually, though, Martin tired of the construction business and began looking for a way out. He learned about the field of home inspection through a contractor he was working for at the time.

As Martin's interest grew, and he contemplated starting his own business, his employer reacted unfavorably. "He found out I was planning on it and fired me on the spot because there was a conflict of interest. So all of a sudden, I was unemployed and had a new baby girl. I read all the books I could on home inspection. I got business cards printed up and started by being the least expensive home inspector [in my area]. It snowballed, but it took a long time, and it wasn't easy. Fortunately, I was still sort of in and out of the acting, and I was working for other people doing construction work. I [also] had unemployment insurance going at the time. It finally got to the point where I didn't have to do anything but home inspection and was able to work full time at it."

Crawford, a board member of NAHI—an association established to help promote and develop the home inspection industry—was a home remodeler before he entered the inspection business. "I had my own business," he says. "Then I went to work for a large, well-known remodeling firm. While there, back in 1986, I realized there was going to be a home inspection industry. It looked attractive, so I took steps to get some information and opened a home inspection division for the home remodeling company."

Fred B.'s partner, Brenda R., says their motivation for getting into home inspection was to get Fred "out of doing heavy construction work when he turned 50." According to Brenda, Fred had done carpentry and remodeling for many years, so home inspection was a perfect business that would let him use some of the experience and knowledge he had gained in those fields. "I think that's a motivation for a lot of people to get into this business," says Brenda, who, with Fred, has a home inspection business based in Seattle.

Frank J., a home inspector based in Carson City, Nevada, says his reasons for getting into the business were based on the frustration he felt after buying his first home. "After I bought my first house—which I never had inspected—I realized that there were a lot of things that could go wrong," says Frank. "That's basically why I got into [the business]. I had problems with my own house. If I had had it inspected beforehand, believe me, the offer would have been a lot different. It also gave me a chance to check out different aspects of building."

Scott Clements, the public relations director for the California Real Estate Inspection Association (CREIA)s, was introduced to the home inspection business while working for a

> **Tip...**
>
> **Smart Tip**
>
> According to the Small Business Administration, there are four basics of success in small business: sound management practices, industry experience, technical support, and planning ability.

franchisor in their corporate office. "Later," he says, "I got into the home inspection business as an inspector, owning and operating my own company [a franchise]." For Clements, the best things about the home inspection business are: "You get to be out in the open, you get to set your own hours, and you get to work with the public. And, of course, there are the compensation opportunities."

Robert W., a home inspector in Charlotte, North Carolina, got some training to prepare for his career in home inspection and feels it was the best thing he ever did. "I went to a school in Washington, DC, for a week," Robert says. "They told you how to inspect, what you're looking at, what to inspect. They also went over a lot of different marketing ideas you could do—how to get business, how to set it up. It was very helpful."

Woody L. got interested in the home inspection business after his brother opened a home inspection franchise. Woody says he always knew that he would have a business of his own someday; he just didn't know what.

"My wife and I talked about it quite a bit," he says. "I had a cushy job in advertising sales and had built the department up from nothing to where I was making a six-figure income. I had five weeks paid vacation every year. We had always been really careful with our money, had our cars paid off and money in the bank. We lived below our means and took advantage of the company stock plan and 401(k). The company treated me very well, and I got along with everyone. But I knew every year they'd rework the quotas and the compensation plan so I had to bring in lots more revenue to earn the same amount of money. Everybody's heard the line 'You can be replaced.' I was never happy in my career until I realized it was a two-way street, that 'they' could be replaced every bit as much as I could."

The Right Stuff

Entering the home inspection field is a great ground-floor opportunity. As is the case with any new business—especially one where the market outlook is so healthy—competition can be fierce. As a result, you will need to be up to the challenge.

Since the first home inspections that were performed in the early 1970s, the home inspectors that have risen to the top are those individuals who possess some specific personality traits, in addition to technical and business expertise. Let's take a look at what these include.

Limber Up

One of the foremost attributes you'll need as a home inspector is flexibility. Why? The home inspection industry can't exactly be labeled "static." The home inspection

Business Basics from the SBA

The Small Business Administration (SBA) recommends doing a pre-business checklist. The answers to a number of key questions, according to the SBA, "will help you create a focused, well-researched business plan that should serve as a blueprint. It should detail how your business will be operated, managed, and capitalized."

For their comprehensive checklist of first steps to take when considering going into business for yourself, visit the SBA's web site at www.sba.gov/starting. From the menu bar on the left, choose "Your First Steps." You will find a questionnaire designed to help you focus your entrepreneurial aspirations. The topics covered include: why you want to go into business for yourself, what type of business you want to start, what demand your business will fill, and, finally, a pre-business checklist covering everything from choosing a name to determining the financing you'll need.

industry almost always parallels what's occurring in the real-estate world, so when homes are selling, the home inspector is working a lot. When homes are not selling, the inspector is not working as much—and sometimes not at all.

Entrepreneurs in the home inspection business must be prepared for these ups and downs and be able to adjust their businesses accordingly. Some of the home inspectors interviewed for this book say they live off their savings during down times. Others have been flexible enough to develop secondary sources of income to help sustain them during dry times. For example, Darrell H., a home inspector in Seattle, and Bob Mulloy, the home inspector in East Bridgewater, Massachusetts, got into teaching home inspection classes and write articles for various publications.

Generally Speaking

The ability to function as a "generalist" is another important trait for a home inspector. In this industry, it means knowing a little something about everything having to do with homes and home inspecting. You will need to understand all the components in a building and the relationships between different systems. You'll need to be familiar with the real-estate industry. You should also have good written and verbal communication skills—not to mention knowledge of how to operate a small business.

Brenda R., the home inspector from Seattle, believes there is tremendous value to having some sort of hands-on experience. "If a problem is found," she says, "[the home inspector] is able to let the client know if it's a minor thing and if they're able to fix it themselves. There's a lot of that kind of background, where it's not just identifying a problem but helping [the homeowner] solve it."

Crawford, an NAHI board member, acknowledges that while it's always helpful for a home inspector to have some background in the trades (such as remodeling, engineering, or home rehabilitation), it's not always necessary in his opinion. "With proper training," says Crawford, "the other important attributes can carry a person right into the industry." And just what are these other attributes?

> **Stat Fact**
> According to the American Society of Home Inspectors, 81 percent of inspectors consider home inspection their full-time profession. The average home inspector is 49 years old and has been in the business for about eight years.

Down to Specifics

Crawford ranks communication skills first, both verbal and written. "Many home inspectors do not present themselves well and then recognize eventually that their phone's not ringing," he says. Crawford also says this happens when an inspector unnecessarily alarms their client by painting a picture of futility if a house has problems, rather than putting the problems into proper perspective. "It's a very important line that an inspector has to walk in terms of how their information is presented fairly," he emphasizes.

Mulloy agrees: "A home inspector should have a background in dealing with the public in a service capacity. He or she must have an analytical, inquisitive mind, and a willingness to listen and learn. And most important, a home inspector must be a trained observer who can recognize the telltale signs of problems and then convey that knowledge to a client in a manner that is objective and unbiased." In addition, he notes, an inspector should be literate, articulate, and computer savvy.

According to Crawford, NAHI recommends that prospective home inspectors develop their interpersonal skills so that they can deal successfully with the amount of client contact that's involved in this field. Since everyone from the buyer to the seller to the real-estate agent has a different agenda in the home inspection process, tempers (as well as lawsuits) can flare if situations are not handled in a professional and tactful manner.

In addition, it's also important for home inspectors to be able to communicate effectively in writing since they must routinely report their findings in written reports—documents which often become key in real-estate transactions. According to Crawford, the goal for the home inspector is to enter the purchase process; give a knowledgeable, objective assessment of the home's condition at the time it's inspected;

and then leave the process without incurring subsequent liability. Communicating in a precise manner is essential to reduce liability and the risk of lawsuits (see Chapter 4 for information on errors and omissions insurance).

Sixth Sense

A natural curiosity is important for the prospective home inspector, says franchisee Woody L. "You've got to use all of your senses when inspecting," he says. "Naturally, you use your eyes, but you have to use your other senses, too." For instance, he notes, ask yourself if the floor sounds funny or feels different when you walk across the room. Or when you first go into a basement, ask yourself if you smell anything. Moldy, mildew smells, he advises, may be your only clue that there's a leaky basement.

Mulloy recommends that the prospective home inspector not be afraid of "heights, tight, dirty places, or nasty critters." Can you climb ladders with no problem? What about those hard-to-reach areas? Will you be able to crawl into that tight crawl space? And are you physically fit? Remember, you'll be checking for as much as you can in a home. These are questions you need to ask yourself before getting into this field.

If you simply enjoy almost everything to do with home construction, home repair, rattling around in old houses (or new for that matter), then home inspection should prove to be a fun, ideal business for you! If you're not sure that you have all the "right stuff" for the industry, but you know you have the interest, consider filling in the gaps by getting some additional training and practice.

Now that we've covered the basics, we'll take a look at what constitutes a good foundation for your home inspection business.

2

The
Foundation

Before getting into any business, including home inspection, it's essential to find out if there is a strong market for the product or service you will provide. In order to do this, you will have to research as much about your prospective market as possible. Based on what you find, you will have to determine if there will be room for you and your business in the existing market.

Thorough market research is crucial to the success of your business. In this chapter, we'll look at how to approach market research. We'll also look at how it can help you as you draw up your business plan and the mission statement for your business.

Survey Says . . .

As you begin your market research, think about the fundamentals you will need to know in order to assess whether your business can be successful in your area. We've provided a "Market Research Survey" on page 14 to get you thinking. For starters, you'll want to know the population in the area where you will do business and the annual home sales figures in your area. You should also find out how many permits were issued for new home construction in your area. In addition to these kinds of demographics, you'll need to know what type of competition you will face. How many home inspectors are in your area? Are they franchisees or independents? How successful are they?

The U.S. Census Bureau, the U.S. Dept. of Housing and Urban Development (HUD), the Small Business Administration's (SBA) web site (www.sba.gov/starting/index research.html), and your local library are all good places to start when gathering demographic information. If you don't want to go it alone, you can contact your state, regional, or local economic development agency for assistance. In many cases, these agencies have already collected and analyzed data that may be useful to you. There are also demographic service companies in the private sector, which provide demographic reports for a fee. Try searching the internet to locate private demographic services, or ask for a referral from the professional associations you join.

Market Share

Who will your customers be? Besides homebuyers and sellers, your customer base may include warranty companies and banks. Warranty companies offer homebuyers policies to cover any unforeseen home repairs. As an added service, as well as being in the warranty company's best interests, the company will hire home inspectors to take a look at the home being covered. Banks also have a vested interest in the condition of a home since they are lending the homebuyer money.

As a new home inspector, your competition will be other home inspectors in the area, both independents and franchisees. It will be your job to effectively compete in this arena for jobs, so it's a good idea to know as much as you can about the companies you're up against. One way to do this is simply to consult your local Yellow Pages and see how many companies or individuals are listed under the heading "Home Inspection." But don't stop there. Find out if they're well-established. Do they offer the same services as you at the same or lower price?

Sizing Up the Market

Your clientele doesn't have to be limited to homebuyers. According to Inspectit.com, the web site of the American Home Inspectors Training Insitute which provides information and products to home inspectors, the following are other individuals or groups likely to need the services of a home inspector:

○ *Home sellers.* They may be interested in pre-listing inspections to find any problems before putting a house on the market.

○ *Homeowners.* They'll need to know the condition of their home before contracting for repairs.

○ *Relocation services.* These services need to know a home's condition before they purchase property for corporate employees.

○ *Owners who are renovating or building a house.* They may want an inspector to watch out for their interests during construction.

○ *Commercial property buyers.* Real-estate investors or retail store owners may need to make sure a building they are buying is in good condition.

The more you know about your competition, the better you will be able to determine if you can get a substantial piece of the market share. You will have to assess whether there are too many home inspectors in your general area. What might be too many for one business owner might not be for another more enterprising individual.

If you believe there is an overabundance of inspectors in your area, you have two options: Either choose to operate in another location, or stay in your own if you believe you can provide better service or something additional that your competitors do not. For instance, you might be able to compete if you offer special services (such as radon, air quality, or asbestos testing). You'll need to determine whether there is, in fact, a market for the special services you consider offering. Knowing your competition will also help you in deciding how to price your services competitively.

According to the SBA, "The principles of determining market share and market potential are the same for all geographic areas. First,

Smart Tip

Tip...

As a business owner, it will be your task to know your customer base. Identify and describe your target market by age, sex, income, education level, profession, and type of residence. Once you've identified your target market, you can concentrate your limited marketing budget just on those customers who are most likely to purchase your service.

Market Research Survey

As part of your market research, you should ask yourself the following questions to determine if the area you plan to work in is suitable for your business:

What is the population in my area? _____

_____

What are annual home sale figures in this region? _____

_____

How many permits were issued for new construction in the previous year?

_____

How many home inspectors are in this area? _____

_____

What kinds of services and pricing do they offer? _____

_____

What percentage of the market have they acquired? _____

_____

Will I be able to do enough business in this region to be successful? _____

_____

In addition, research the following before starting your business:

❏ Analyze your start-up costs, as well as the ongoing monthly expenses you anticipate.

❏ Investigate professional organizations, both nationally and locally.

❏ Find out what licenses/permits are required. Look into your state's regulations pertaining to home inspection.

❏ Get to know your local real-estate community.

❏ Determine what segment of the market you will target (i.e., what types of customers will want to pay for your services).

❏ Determine which extra services you will offer. For example, determine if there is a market in your area for lead paint, septic tank, or well-water testing.

determine a customer profile (who) and the geographic size of the market (how many). This is the general market potential. Knowing the number and strength of your competitors (and then estimating the share of business you will take from them) will give you the market potential specific to your enterprise."

If you're feeling overwhelmed at the prospect of handling this research task on your own, you may want to consider hiring a market research firm to help you—provided you have the funds. These firms can be expensive and usually charge upwards of $200 or more per project.

Franchise or Independent?

You have several options to consider as you contemplate starting a business. Will you buy a franchise, an existing business, or start your own business independently?

If you feel comfortable going it alone and prefer to have direct control of your business, you will likely choose to operate as an independent. By choosing this route, you will be entirely responsible for designing your own inspection routine, as well as your pre-inspection agreements and reports. One of the advantages of this option is that you won't need as much start-up capital as a franchisee will. On a six-month basis, low-end start-up can be as little as $5,000. This is, of course, if you decide you can start as a homebased business and do without all the "bells and whistles," like high-priced software packages and elaborate home inspection equipment. At the high end, start-up costs for an independent could reach between $20,000 and $30,000.

If you decide to go the independent route, you have another option to consider. Would you prefer to buy an existing business, with a customer base and cash flow already in place? Or would you rather start your own business from the ground up? Again, this will depend on your comfort level and interests as a business owner, as well as the availability of businesses for sale in your area. If you don't want the uncertainty of starting a business from scratch and wondering if it will take off, you might consider buying an existing business. On the other hand, if you're not willing to take on the potential problems of a previous owner, and if you prefer to create your own systems and see your business through the start-up stages, then starting your own business may be the option for you.

Alternatively, you might select the franchise route because you don't have much solid business

 Beware!
It's easy to overestimate on sales projections for your business, as well as underestimate costs. There will always be unforeseen problems or items you've overlooked. So forecast your projected income as conservatively as possible, while allowing for additional expenses. And make sure you keep extra cash in reserve.

experience or experience in the field you want to enter. Having the support of a franchise helps eliminate some of that concern. Even though a successful franchise nets smaller profit margins on average than an independent (because of franchising fees and expenses), the odds of surviving in the business as a franchisee are usually better.

Woody L., a franchisee in Glendale, Arizona, says he barely knew the home inspection business existed until his brother opened a franchise in Portland, Oregon. "He sounded like a little kid at Christmas the day he told me he was quitting his job and becoming a home inspector," Woody says. "I watched him grow his business the first year, talked with him often about how it was going, and he was just as enthusiastic a year into it as he had been day one."

Woody chose the franchise route because it provided established routines, training, and support that would enable him to operate in a way that was already proven to be successful. Another reason some home inspectors go the franchise route is that they can benefit from a company's name recognition. According to the International Franchise Association, the more recognized the name, the more likely it will draw customers who know its products or services.

While buying a franchise may reduce your investment risk by enabling you to associate with an established company, it can be costly. Estimated start-up costs for a home inspection franchise can run the gamut, anywhere from $15,000 to $40,000, depending on the location and how assertive the owner is during negotiations. Besides fees to the franchisor, there are also often minimum investment requirements. It is also likely that you will have to relinquish a significant amount of control over your business, since you have to operate your business in the manner the franchisor has already set up.

If you decide to go this route, do your homework before buying a franchise. Find out more about the franchise's reputation. Hop onto the internet and see what's been written about the company. Is there a history of dissatisfaction among its franchisees? Have lawsuits been brought by franchisees against the franchisor? Finally, talk with as many franchisees as you can.

Got a Plan?

A solid business plan is essential to the success of your business. Your business plan will precisely define your business, and identify your goals and how you'll achieve those goals. Your business plan will be an important document

Smart Tip

Tip...

If you're not the type of person who relishes the work involved in drawing up a business plan or market research survey, try thinking of it this way: Wouldn't it be nice to do a little advanced planning before starting a business, rather than encounter problems once you're underway?

when you go to get funding for your start-up. Bank officials usually ask to see one during loan discussions. Likewise, any investors you may approach will also want to see a business plan.

Your business plan should include financial documents such as a balance sheet, income statement, and cash-flow analysis.

The Name Game

When you go into business, you will likely need to choose a fictitious business name—referred to as a dba ("doing business as")—and register that name with your city, county, or state. This applies if you intend to call your business anything other than your own name. Many home inspectors like to adhere to a standard rule of thumb taught in many business courses—that you should select a business name that describes in some way the service you will offer. That way, you give the public a clear idea of what your company is all about.

Another good rule of thumb is to make sure the name is meaningful. Does it communicate the objectives and values of your business? Start brainstorming by listing ideas that relate to your company's services, values, location, and anything that sets your company apart from the competition.

When you've come up with a few ideas, see if any of them meet the following criteria:

- Is the name easy to pronounce and understand (even over the phone)?
- Have you checked to make sure the name isn't already taken? (Start by looking through the Yellow Pages; then check with your local business authority.)
- Will the name fit on a business card?
- Is a similar URL available? (Check with Network Solutions, at its web site, www.networksolutions.com, to make sure the domain name you have in mind is not already registered.)

On a Mission

A thoughtful, well-written mission statement can serve as a touchstone for your business. You can come back to it time and time again to help you get your bearings whenever you face a difficult business decision or whenever you lose sight of why you made the choice to go into the home inspection business in the first place. A mission statement also provides your employees with a clear vision of what working at your company is all about.

We've provided a worksheet on page 19 to get you started on drafting a mission statement for your business. A good place to start is to ask yourself what you want to offer your clients. Maybe it's dedication, respect for the customer, providing information and education to your clients, or even delivering timely reports. A mission statement should:

- Give a broad description of what you do and what your company does.
- Describe with whom or for whom you do it.
- Describe how you do it better or more effectively than anyone else.
- Tell why you do it.

Once you've come up with your list, incorporate the items into paragraph form. Keep refining the paragraph until it reflects who you are and what you want your business to stand for.

On Location

It's perfectly acceptable for home inspectors to work out of their homes, so the matter of location becomes a matter of whether a leased office space is really necessary for doing business, at least initially. This is entirely a subjective decision for every home inspector. Would you prefer to minimize your start-up costs and your ongoing monthly expenses by starting out as a homebased business? Or is it unrealistic to think that you'll actually get the quiet or space at home that you'll need to develop a professional business operation?

Many home inspectors work out of their homes and enjoy the overhead cost savings. They usually have a family member answering the phones and helping out with the bookkeeping, which helps cut costs in those two areas. But that doesn't mean you shouldn't set a budget. You will need to find out how much you can comfortably afford to spend on things such as furniture and equipment. Don't forget to budget for items like electrical wiring, carpentry, additional phone lines, and supplies for the office.

Also make sure your home office offers enough space and privacy so you can effectively conduct business. There's no denying that there can be many distractions at home, so it's important that you keep your home office just that—an office space. Keep it as professional-looking as possible. Let family and friends know to keep interruptions to a minimum while you're working. Even if you don't have clients coming in, you are still a business owner and need to have this space for yourself.

Tip...

Smart Tip
Homebased businesses are popular because of reduced expenses and lower overhead costs.

Drafting Your Mission Statement

Use this worksheet to get started on drafting a mission statement for your business. Answer the following items and then consolidate the responses you feel are most important into a paragraph or two summarizing your company's mission.

Describe what your company does.

_____

_____

What clientele will you serve?

_____

_____

In what location(s) will you do business?

_____

_____

How is your company unique (i.e., how do you differ from the competition)?

_____

_____

What are your company's primary goals?

_____

_____

_____

What values are central to your business?

_____

_____

_____

If you use part of your home regularly and exclusively as an office, there is the highly coveted home office tax break come tax time. You may be entitled to deduct a portion of your mortgage, rent, and/or utilities, as well as advertising costs, supplies, equipment, legal and professional services, and vehicle mileage. Remember to keep accurate records and receipts for all expenses having to do with your business, including a mileage log for your car. For more information, check with your local IRS office or a professional accountant.

Stat Fact
According to the Small Business Administration, experts estimate that as many as 20 percent of new small-business enterprises are operated out of the owner's home.

Movin' on Up

Many home inspectors are homebased in the beginning, only to find that after working hard and growing their business for a number of years, they either need an office location or are finally able to afford one. Obtaining a storefront location can be an exciting and heady time for a new business owner—but don't lose your head (or get in over your head, for that matter). A good thing to do while you are still in the planning stages for a move to a leased office space is to formulate a small survey form to examine the pros and cons of moving your business location.

You should start by asking yourself:

- What area do I want to be in?
- Can I afford the leases in this particular area?
- Is this a safe area or known for high crime rate?
- Does this location allow me enough space?
- Is this space large enough if I add employees?
- What will my commute be like?
- Is there enough parking for employees and customers?
- Do I need to be close to a freeway?
- What is the landlord like?
- What are the typical costs for heating, air conditioning, and electricity?

You might also want to sketch out a design of your prospective office space. This will help you to see how much room you will need for everything and everyone you want included in the space.

The
Cost Factor

Don't let the title of this chapter scare you off. Getting started in the home inspection business can cost as little as $5,000, according to the home inspectors and experts interviewed for this book. Some said it was possible to work from home and just hang out your shingle. However, you can spend substantially more if you plan to offer special types of testing services (for which you'll need equipment), or if you elect to have a leased office space and employees rather than working out of your home and enlisting the help of family members. In this chapter, we'll take a look at the kinds of start-up costs you can expect as you begin your own home inspection business.

Start-Up Costs

Whether you are working out of your home or leasing an office, the items you most likely cannot do without in the home inspection business include computer hardware and software, stationery, business cards, forms, and printing paper—in addition to a well-running car and basic tools.

Although he doesn't include a vehicle in his list of start-up costs, Bob Mulloy, in East Bridgewater, Massachusetts, says "having a fairly nice-looking, working vehicle is important for the home inspector. A home inspector should own a vehicle that portrays the curb appeal of a professional. Seeing a home inspector pull up to the home in a broken-down pickup truck would not create a very good impression," he adds. "So you must factor a fairly new car, truck, or van into the [business] equation."

Darrell H. in Seattle takes a more frugal approach to the items you need to get started. "In a literal sense," he says, "all you really need is a flashlight and a screwdriver. You can do it for as little as that. When I began, I had some marketing costs, which I found were a waste. You can go to education seminars till the cows come home, so you can spend as much as you want. Or buy into a franchise and buy a van. With all this stuff, you can spend $50,000. It depends on what you want to do."

As mentioned in the last chapter, if you are going the franchise route, your start-up costs will be anywhere from $15,000 to $40,000, depending on the franchise you choose. For an independently run business, which we will focus on in this chapter, you should figure on $5,000 up to $30,000 to get started. According to NAHI's (National Association of Home Inspectors) Executive Director Mallory Anderson, home inspectors should probably plan on a $5,000 initial reserve for the first six months of business. What will your start-up costs include? Refer to the "Your Company's Start-Up Expenses" worksheet on page 34 as you read through the following discussion of start-up expenses.

Getting Educated

Your first steps toward starting your own business will be investigating the market and investing in educational courses related to home inspection. Learning about the market will involve reading trade journals and other publications, and joining professional associations. Factor in approximately $20 to $100 per year for subscriptions to

Beware!
One of the leading causes of business failure is insufficient start-up capital. You should allow six-months' worth of operating expenses as your suggested operating capital, and you should work closely with your accountant to estimate your cash flow needs.

trade journals or other publications. Budget approximately $100 to $300 yearly for association dues. These costs will depend on which associations you join, as well as how many.

At minimum, it would be wise to budget for at least one training class per year, which could run from $50 to several thousand dollars, depending on the method of instruction. For more information on education and training, see Chapter 6.

If you need help conducting market research, there are firms that specialize in this work. In general, market research firms bid by the project, basing their charges on hourly rates. You may end up spending $200 or more per project.

Getting Professional Advice

It is also wise for any new home inspector to retain the services of a lawyer and an accountant or tax advisor. A lawyer can advise you on setting up a legal structure for your business, as well as review the wording on any contracts you plan to have your customers sign, such as a "pre-inspection agreement." It's also important to establish a relationship with a lawyer early on so that you'll be prepared in the event of a legal challenge—for instance, if a customer decides to hold you liable for an oversight. Depending on the area of the country in which you operate, attorney fees can run anywhere from $90 to $300 per hour.

How do you go about choosing a lawyer? You should start by asking any business contacts you have for references. Another option is to contact your local Bar Association. For any prospective lawyers you consider, evaluate whether they have the appropriate experience to meet your needs. Also evaluate whether their fees are reasonable and whether you have a comfortable rapport with that person that will make it possible to work together successfully.

Accountants can provide invaluable services to the new business owner. They can advise you on tax matters and show you how to set up a good bookkeeping system. They can also offer advice on choosing insurance. To find a good accountant, you should ask professionals you know for references or approach your state's Society of Certified Public Accountants for a referral. You may want to consider going with a CPA since this certification guarantees that the accountant has passed a national standardized examination and has proved he or she has the skill set to do the job. Most accounting firms charge fees ranging from $75 to $275 per hour, though you can also hire an accountant on a monthly retainer.

Getting Insured

Insurance for the home inspector most often includes a general liability policy, as well as "errors and omissions" coverage. In addition, if you'll be working out of your home, find out if your existing homeowner's policy will cover business assets/equipment. If not, you may be able to add to your existing coverage for as little as several hundred dollars per year. For general liability and errors and omissions coverage, you can expect to pay in the range of $1,200 to $2,800 per year, depending on the amount of coverage you need. Many home inspection associations offer competitive rates if you join their organization. For more information on insurance for home inspectors, see Chapter 4.

Beware!

According to www.ehomein spect.com, "Asbestos fibers are a health threat when inhaled. The microscopic fibers can become lodged in the respiratory system and lead to asbestosis, or scarring of the respiratory tissues." Plan to take safety courses to learn about dealing with hazardous materials and find out what protective equipment you need to have for handling specific materials.

Supplying Your Office

Your basic office supplies will include paper for your printer, fax, and copier ($25 to $50 per case—10 reams of 500 sheets each); extra print cartridges ($25 to $80); and extra fax cartridges (up to $80). You'll also need a variety of miscellaneous items that you may already have around the house, like file folders, pens, pencils, paperclips, a stapler, scissors, etc. You will also want to stock up on CDs to store electronic files for either your own records or to hand out to customers.

You will need to have business cards, letterhead, and matching envelopes printed up. Plan on spending about $200 to $400 at your local FedEx, Kinko's, or other copier. You can purchase software to do it on your own, but be sure to buy high quality paper to print on to ensure your materials are professional looking. Also factor in the cost of drawing up and printing your own forms, such as billing and report forms.

Bright Idea

Digital cameras have come down considerably in price and are a worthwhile investment for your home inspection business. You can take this small, handheld camera into tight spaces to photograph whatever you want your client to see and print out a copy from your computer to include with your report.

Getting Equipped

Equipment for home inspectors can run the gamut from the absolutely essential to the not-so-essential. However, if you feel a certain piece of equipment will help you do your job better, then it may be worth investing in. Keep in mind that for the first couple years of starting your business, all investments should probably lead toward income-generation. Standard equipment for a home inspector consists of three areas of work-related necessities: basic home inspection tools, computer equipment, and office equipment. There are several other items that may be very useful to have. However, if you are trying to keep your start-up costs to a minimum, you may decide these don't need to be on your critical list: a digital camera, a copier, new office furniture, and tools for specialized services.

We've provided a checklist of equipment for your home inspection business on pages 30 and 31. Use this worksheet to calculate how much you will need to spend for each type of equipment listed.

Tool Basics

Basic tools for the home inspector include: a ladder, flashlight, tape measure, hammer, screwdriver, level and square, binoculars, stud finder, electrical tester, telescoping mirror, water pressure gauge, carbon monoxide detector, step ladder, thermometer, probe, gloves, and coveralls. A low-end estimate for basic home inspection tools is around $60 to $200.

When asked about the equipment he uses, Robert W. in Charlotte, North Carolina, reiterated many of the items listed above. "You have to have a good flashlight," he says. "You also need screwdrivers, thermometers, probes, and electrical testers. I have gloves and coveralls [in case] I go under houses. You need a good ladder to go up on the roof and stepladders so you can go into attics. A lot of attics don't have pull-down stairs. I also have a digital camera so I can take pictures. And cell phones are good so you can stay in contact with people."

Computer Equipment Basics

If you don't already have computer hardware and software, your start-up costs should be adjusted to include these items. Having a computer is practically a necessity in any business, and the home inspection industry is no exception. Many home inspectors opt for laptop or handheld computers that they can take along on inspections to generate reports for clients on the spot. Handheld computers can even be taken along while inspecting such hard-to-reach places as attics and crawl spaces. If you note a problem or defect, you can enter it immediately so you won't forget. Laptop or notebook computers cost an average of $1,000 to $2,500, and it will cost you about $400 to $1,000 for a handheld PC.

If you decide on a desktop PC, these days you can get a great Pentium class system with plenty of hard drive capacity, monitor, modem, and mouse, the latest version of Microsoft Vista, at least 64MB RAM, a CD-ROM drive and/or Zip drive, and wireless modem for surfing the internet and downloading files, plus printer (either an inkjet or laser model) for not much more than $1,000. The benefit of a computer for the home inspector includes direct inspections-related software but also software programs and packages to aid in almost every aspect of business operations. There's enough on any new home inspector's mind without having to worry about how to maintain the books, pay the bills, or write the reports. Fortunately, there are a variety of software programs to assist you in these areas:

- *Reporting software.* By all accounts, the narrative-style report is becoming the standard in the home inspection industry. There are many software packages on the market today to help a home inspector generate this style of report, so take your time and research which program will work best for you.

  Several examples of reporting software packages include: InspectIt's ReportPlus 2001, which costs $750 (www.inspectit.com); Home Inspection 2000, priced at $195 (www.homeinspection2000.com); and Report Writer from 3-D Inspection System (www.3dinspection.com), which runs $199 (all prices as of this writing). Take advantage of the free demos that many companies will allow you to download, or free or low-cost CDs that they will send you. This way, you can try out several kinds of reporting software and compare how well each meets your specific needs, as well as how user-friendly they are. Keep in mind that some reporting software packages have basic computer system requirements, so note what they are and be sure you have a compatible computer for the software you choose.

- *Accounting/data entry software.* If you've been fretting over how you will handle the financial end of things, there are a number of accounting and data entry programs that can help you run your business smoothly. You can even find software for order-taking, invoicing, labeling, mapping, client database support, cost-tracking, and marketing—not to mention letter-mailing and scheduling software.

One way to determine what program(s) you'll want to go with is to go to your local office supply store, or visit it via the web, and compare the accounting and data entry software packages being offered. Ultimately, your decision will depend on your needs and budget.

Smart Tip

According to the Small Business Administration, most suppliers want new accounts. A prime source for finding suppliers is the Thomas Register of American Manufacturers (Thomas Register), which lists manufacturers by categories and geographic area. You can visit their web site at www.thomas net.com. Most libraries also have a directory of manufacturers listed by state. If you know a product's manufacturer, a letter or phone call to the company will get you the local distributor-wholesaler.

Some general accounting programs include Intuit Quicken Home and Business, Intuit QuickBooks, and Peachtree Accounting, running between $70 and $500. You may also choose to purchase a spreadsheet program to help you keep track of various client and billing records. Microsoft Excel and Lotus 1-2-3 are basic spreadsheet programs you can purchase for around $250.

Office Equipment Basics

A good phone system is a necessity for your office. For a two-line speakerphone with auto-redial, memory dial, a mute button, and other features, you'll spend in the range of $150. If you are working out of your home, you should consider getting a second line to use exclusively for your business. Your local phone company will charge around $40 to $60 for line installation.

Many home inspectors also find that a cellular phone is indispensable. Expect to pay in the neighborhood of $100 for a cellular phone, though many times it comes free when you sign up for service and sign on to a one- or two-year contract. Be sure you shop around and compare rates before you decide on a cellular phone carrier.

You'll also need an answering machine or voice mail to take messages when you are out doing a home inspection or are otherwise unavailable. Plan on spending an additional $35 to $65 for a basic answering machine, or $6 to $20 per month for voice mail.

A fax machine is another of the equipment basics you'll need. A plain paper fax machine will cost you under a hundred dollars, or you might opt to go with a multifunction device with a fax/copier/printer/scanner ranging anywhere from $250 to $800. While these multifunction devices do give you a certain degree of flexibility, be aware that they may not be suitable for large copy jobs, which you may be better off taking to the local print shop or running off on a dedicated copier.

Not on the Critical List

You may spend much more on your equipment start-up costs if you elect to purchase home inspection tools for specialized services. The types of specialized services you may choose to offer, as well as the equipment needed, are discussed in Chapter 6.

There are a number of sources you can consult for home inspection equipment. You can start on the internet with Professional Equipment (www.professionalequipment.com), Inspection Tools Unlimited (www.inspectioncentral.com), or Inspector Tools (www.inspectortools.com). In addition to standard categories, such as electrical, gas analyzers and detectors, moisture testing, hand tools, and safety equipment, you will also find specialized equipment for services such as radon gas testing and lead paint testing.

Here's a sample of the types of equipment available from Professional Equipment, based in Hauppauge, New York:

- Circuit analysis: 9-volt battery, circuit locator and tester, breaker locator
- Discovery: borescopes, concrete sounders, liquid and gas leak detectors, metal/voltage/stud detectors, pipe and cable locators, waste leak detectors, metallic scanners
- Electrical: AC/DC clamp meters, analog earth resistance testers, oscilloscopes, power analyzer testers, voltage indicators
- Gas detection: gas detectors, carbon monoxide detectors, gas leak detectors
- Humidity: humidity measurement systems, thermo-hygrometers, temperature/humidity/dew point/thermometers
- Heating, ventilation, and air conditioning (HVAC): fluorite anemometers, air flow meters, HVAC analyzers, electronic manometers, thermo-anemometers, refrigerant gas
- Measuring: crack monitors, depth gauges, magnifiers, pocket handyman, laser measures, electronic distance measurers
- Lighting: flashlights, bulbs, battery packs
- Temperature: digital and laser thermometers, infrared sensors, temperature data loggers with software, waterproof pocket thermometers

If that isn't enough, there are still other items a home inspector could make good use of, such as smoke alarm testers, tub stoppers, disposable coveralls, and carrying cases and digital cameras to photograph the home inspection. Digital cameras are extremely popular with home inspectors because they can be carried along during the inspection process and taken into small, tight spaces. Many inspectors like to use digital cameras so that they can immediately document an area of a home and use the photos to explain things to their clients. Expect to pay in the range of $400 to $700 for a good quality digital camera.

Although not on the list of necessities, you may want to consider purchasing a simple photocopier for your office. A desktop copier will run you $400 or less, while a stand-alone model will cost about $500 to $800. And you may want new office furniture. Basic office furniture for your homebased office will include a computer work center or desk, chair, printer stand, filing cabinets, and a bookcase. If you can make do with items that you already have around the house, you'll be able to keep your start-up costs to a minimum. However, if you think you will

Beware!
Lead-based paint is a concern in most homes built before 1978. White lead was used extensively as a pigment in paint until the rising cost of lead in the 1960s prompted the use of other pigments. The growing awareness of lead poisoning resulted in the eventual ban of lead-based paint in 1978.

need to supplement what you have with a few new pieces, here's a range of what you can expect to pay. For a basic computer work center, you will pay around $200, while a midrange desk may run you from $200 to $300. A printer stand will cost $50 to $75, two-drawer letter-size filing cabinets $25 to $100, and a four-shelf bookcase about $70.

Office chairs range from $60 to $250 or more, depending on the features you're after. Although an inspector won't spend as much time sitting in an office chair as some professions, spring for a comfortable, ergonomic one. After a long day in the field, you will welcome a comfortable chair in which to sit as you write up your report.

Surfing the Net

Along with your nifty new computer (or the old one you already have), you'll need to get internet access. You can go through one of the many internet service providers out there, such as America Online or Earthlink, and get access to e-mail and the web for about $20 per month. However, you will probably want to go with high-speed broadband internet service; it just makes more sense for any business.

In the internet age, it's no wonder that many inspectors choose to have a web site in order to give their business a presence in cyberspace. If you already happen to have expertise in the area of web site design, or you're lucky enough to have a friend or family member that does, you're ahead of the game. Otherwise, your best bet is to hire a professional web site designer. For a fairly conservative site, without too many graphics or effects, expect to pay in the range of $300 to $500 for hands-on help from a designer. If you decide to add lots of "bells and whistles" to your site, however, web site design can run into the thousands of dollars.

And your web site will need to be hosted—a server with the capability to handle web traffic and keep your site available 24/7 to prospective customers. For basic web hosting services, you can expect to pay from $10 to $75 per month.

Putting It All Together

We've provided a worksheet on page 34, "Your Company's Start-Up Expenses," so that you can estimate the projected start-up costs for your own home inspection business. For an idea of what your start-up costs may look like, see the costs for two hypothetical home inspection businesses on pages 32 and 33. The hypothetical companies include Do-It-Right Home Inspection and Pro Inspect. The owner of Do-It-Right Home Inspection works out of his home, which saves on overhead costs such as rent and utilities. He currently has no employees. Pro Inspect's owner has leased office space and employs several part-time employees, at a pay rate of $12 per hour.

Equipment Basics

Use this worksheet to calculate the cost of equipment for your home inspection business. Enter the totals in the "Your Company's Start-Up Expenses" worksheet on page 34.

Basic Home Inspection Tools

Ladder	$ _____
Stepladder	_____
Flashlight	_____
Tape measure	_____
Hammer	_____
Screwdriver	_____
Level/square	_____
Binoculars	_____
Stud finder	_____
Electrical tester	_____
Telescoping mirror	_____
Water pressure gauge	_____
Carbon monoxide detector	_____
Thermometer	_____
Probe	_____
Gloves	_____
Coveralls	_____
Total	$ _____

Computer Equipment

Computer system (with modem, hard drive, monitor, and mouse)	_____
Or:	
Laptop computer or handheld PC	_____
Inkjet or laser printer	_____
Surge protector	_____
UPS	_____
Software	_____
Total	$ _____

Equipment Basics, continued

Office Equipment

Cellular phone _____

Telephone _____

Answering machine (or voice mail) _____

Fax _____

Calculator _____

Total $ _____

Noncritical Items

Digital camera _____

Copier _____

Office furniture _____

Tools for Special Services _____

Total $ _____

Other

_____

_____

_____

Grand Total $ _____

Home Inspection Start-Up Expenses

Below we've provided an example of what start-up costs might look like for your first six months. We've used two hypothetical home inspection companies—both are independently-run businesses. One is a low-end estimate; the other a high-end approximation of what start-up costs look like for a home inspection business.

The owner of Do-It-Right Home Inspection works out of his home, which saves on overhead costs such as rent and utilities. He already owns a vehicle in good working order and a basic computer system, and only had to invest in new software. He currently has no employees. Pro Inspect's owner rented an office space and bought a new computer system and printer, as well as office equipment, including a fax and copier. She already had a vehicle suitable for business use, and she employs two part-time employees at a pay rate of $12 per hour.

Expenses	Do-It-Right	Pro Inspect
Legal and accounting services	$375	$600
Licenses/permits	$200	$200
Association dues	$100	$500
Market research (including subscriptions)	$150	$200
Training courses:		
Books	$100	$500
Home study materials	$200	$1,000
Tuition	$1000	$5,000
Insurance (six months, general liability/errors and omissions)	$750	$1,000

Home Inspection Start-Up Expenses, continued

Expenses	Do-It-Right	Pro Inspect
Equipment:		
Computer hardware/software	$700	$4,000
Office equipment	$200	$2,000
Basic home inspection tools	$60	$200
Specialized and/or noncritical equipment	$100	$850
Office supplies and printing	$250	$500
Advertising/marketing	$100	$500
Phone (installation and line charges)	$90	$115
Cellular phone service	$50	$100
Internet access	$20	$20
Web page design	$0	$500
Web site hosting	$0	$50
Web advertising	$0	$500
Rent (first month and security deposit)	$0	$1,750
Employee payroll	$0	$960
Total Start-Up Expenses	**$4,445**	**$21,045**

▲

Your Company's Start-Up Expenses

Use this worksheet to estimate your company start-up expenses. You can make copies to work up several scenarios and then compare them to determine which is best for you.

Expenses

Professional association dues	$ _____
Market research (including subscriptions to trade journals)	$ _____
Training courses and materials	$ _____
Legal and accounting services	$ _____
Licenses/permits	$ _____
Insurance	$ _____
Advertising and marketing	$ _____
Office supplies (including printing costs for forms, stationery, envelopes, and business cards)	$ _____

Equipment (Insert totals from "Equipment Basics" worksheet on pages 30 and 31)

Basic home inspection tools	$ _____
Computer equipment	$ _____
Office equipment	$ _____
Specialized and/or noncritical equipment	$ _____
Phone (installation and line charges)	$ _____
Cellular phone service	$ _____
Internet access	$ _____
Web site design	$ _____
Web hosting	$ _____

If your company will not be homebased:

Rent	$ _____
Employee payroll and benefits	$ _____

Total Start-Up Expenses $ _____

4

A Sound
Structure

In order to make sure that your business operates successfully, you will need to create a sound business structure for your company. You will need to decide whether you will run your business as a sole proprietorship, a partnership, or as another legal structure. You will also need to secure general liability insurance and errors and omissions insurance.

In addition, you should check into the permits and licenses you will need to operate in your area, and locate a good lawyer and accountant to call upon when the need arises.

Licenses/Permits

As we've mentioned, many states are just beginning to regulate the home inspection industry. According to the American Society of Home Inspectors (ASHI), there are currently some 31 states with regulations or licensing requirements that apply to home inspection businesses. These states include: Alabama, Arizona, Arkansas, California, Connecticut, Georgia, Louisiana, Maryland, Massachusetts, Montana, Nevada, New Jersey, North Carolina, Oregon, Rhode Island, South Carolina, South Dakota, Tennessee, Texas, and Wisconsin. In addition to these states, the Home Inspection Institute of America lists Pennsylvania and Kentucky (Lexington) in their 2001 list of states that have now regulated home inspection.

The agencies in charge of home inspection regulation and licensing vary from state to state. For instance, in Arizona, the regulator is the State Board of Technical Registration, while in Arkansas, it is the secretary of state's Home Inspector Advisory Board. If you're planning to operate your business in a state that we have not listed here, you should still check into the current licensing requirements in your state. Changes may occur rapidly as this field becomes more regulated.

To keep abreast of changes on the regulatory front, you can consult any industry organizations or associations that you belong to, which should keep up-to-date information on regulatory changes applying to the home inspection industry. And, of course, you should also consult your lawyer to make sure you are current with any licensing requirements necessary for home inspectors in your state.

In addition to the specific licensing that your state may require, don't forget that you will also need to obtain a general business license to operate in your city. Contact your local municipal government to find out how to apply for a business license. The zoning requirements in your area will be checked by the city, and you will need to pay a nominal fee for your business license.

Business Structure

For tax purposes, all self-employed business owners must select a type of legal structure for their businesses. You will likely choose from three options: sole proprietorship, partnership, or corporation. Or you might select from other alternatives, including the S corporation or the limited liability corporation (LLC).

A sole proprietorship is often the easiest structure that a business owner can choose. The profits from the operation of the owner's business are treated as personal income for the purposes of taxation. There is a one-time taxation on all profits, and upon the owner's death, the business is dissolved. A separate tax return and balance sheet are not necessary. However, it is important to remember that a sole proprietor is personally responsible for any debts related to their business. In addition, it may be more difficult to obtain outside funding for a business with this structure.

You may choose to set up your company as a partnership instead. There are two kinds of partnerships—general and limited. General partnerships involve partners that both manage the company and assume responsibility for its debts. Limited partnerships may involve both general partners and limited partners, who act solely as investors.

You may find that it's easier to raise capital as a partnership, and that you have fewer government regulations to contend with than a corporation. The downside is that there are legal risks. You become responsible for the business actions of your partners. You should obtain legal advice and have a partnership agreement in place before deciding on this business structure.

Another option is the corporate structure. Incorporation is considered the most complex of the business structures due to the amount of information you must understand and the number of forms you must submit. The state in which you will operate must permit incorporation. If you are contemplating this step, you will probably want to obtain legal advice. A lawyer can look over incorporation forms, making sure you haven't overlooked any important details.

Side by Side

Fred B. and Brenda R. in Seattle are two home inspectors working as a partnership. Brenda says they function better as a team because there are two of them to go out on inspections. "With most people, there's one guy, and he's trying to look; he's trying to explain; he's trying to do it all. It's very difficult in a short time to try to see everything that you need to see, so we've got the advantage with two of us," she says.

Taking on a partner will change the way your business operates. Before adding a partner, ask yourself a few questions. Are you prepared to share authority for managing your business with someone else? Can you share decision-making? Your partner may have advice and interests different from your own. Are you open to discussing them?

So how do you find that person? A good place to start is with any existing business contacts, especially in the home inspection field. This means you probably already know how well you work together and are familiar with each other's styles. After that, you could approach professional business advisors and intermediaries, such as lawyers, accountants, and consultants. In the end, though, remember to screen all candidates carefully. It's easier to establish trust when you are sure the other person is interested in a partnership. This assures a low risk of the partner eventually becoming a competitor.

Beware!
According to the Small Business Administration, "A business partner does not guarantee success. Personality and character, as well as ability to give technical or financial assistance, determine the ultimate success of a partnership."

Your Lawyer

In a business known to have its fair share of lawsuits, it's a good idea to establish a relationship with a reputable lawyer early on. Preventive legal advice can save you time, trouble, and money. It can also prevent small problems from growing out of control.

Some of the things an attorney can help you with include choosing the right business structure, making sure the proper papers are filed, and drafting and interpreting contracts and leases. If legal action is brought against your business, or if you need to bring legal action against someone else, an attorney is indispensable.

If you don't already have an attorney in mind, ask friends, relatives, or business acquaintances if they know of someone they feel is particularly good. You can also contact your local Bar Association for a list of state bar-certified attorneys in your area, or you can approach your industry trade associations for referrals.

Legal Challenges

"This industry is freaked about lawsuits," says Darrell H., the home inspector in Seattle. "I don't share that [attitude] myself. There are people who have insurance after insurance and disclaimers, and I know a couple different guys who've been sued on a regular basis. I think that gets back to the whole communication thing. What I do is mentally put myself in my buyer's shoes. I say 'OK, what would I want to know about if I were buying this place?' I think a lot of people don't do that," explains Darrell.

Due to the nature of the home inspection industry, the prospect of a lawsuit is a very real possibility. As a result, you must take the appropriate measures to protect yourself—like carrying errors and omissions coverage. But, according to many home inspectors we talked to, you can't let it rule your life.

Fred B. and Brenda R. say they know of a home inspector in their area who got out of the business. He went out of business not because he had lawsuits against his business, but because of the fear that it might happen to him one day.

Legal Eagles

Many lawyers are "general practice" lawyers that handle a wide range of problems and cases, similar to the family doctor. Other lawyers have qualified as "certified specialists" under a state bar program designed to help the public find skilled specialists. If a lawyer is certified, it means he or she has extensive experience and has been tested in a certain area of the law. Certification can take place in criminal law; family law; probate, estate planning and trust law; tax law; workers' compensation; and various types of business law. Be sure you choose a lawyer with the appropriate expertise to help you with the legal needs of your business.

"He had been in the business for nine years or something and had done thousands of inspections," says Brenda. "But he got out because of the fear of client complaints. He actually had fewer complaints than the average home inspector, but it just tears you up every time somebody has a problem. And he was so concerned that he was going to miss something, or [the clients] were going to be unhappy with him that it just wasn't worth it to him."

Common client complaints most often revolve around the home inspector overlooking a potential problem with the house, requiring the customer to shell out money for costly repairs down the road. Another common complaint is that the home inspector and realtor are too closely aligned for comfort. This has become a serious issue in the inspection industry and therefore, as the saying goes, it is best to avoid even the appearance of conflict of interest—working directly with realtors is an important part of the home inspection market, so plan to be clear up front that you will be doing a thorough inspection and revealing everything there is to reveal..

Another common complaint is that the inspector is not articulate enough to convey an accurate assessment of what's going on with the home. Learn how to explain to potential homeowners in language they understand—not construction jargon—the condition of the house, what the priorities are for repairs, and any other realities they will need to face if they were to purchase the home.

Fred B. and Brenda R. say their best defense against potential litigation is to "give the very best possible service to our clients, and, in doing that, we've protected ourselves."

But that doesn't come without sacrifice, according to Brenda. "Personally, in doing that, we've reduced our hourly wage by a significant amount, but we just kind of hope that it averages out. But most people's reality is that they can't really afford to spend that many hours on a house, so they just take that risk that they'll do the best job they can in the limited time that they've got."

Smart Tip

General liability insurance usually covers you for bodily injury, property damage, and advertising injury.

Franchisee Woody L. in Glendale, Arizona, likes the fact that if he runs into complaints from customers or legal action regarding a home inspection, he has his franchise's operations manual and the franchise's home office to go to for advice. "Let's say a complaint comes in," says Woody, "not a big item, but let's say in the $1,000 range. What do you do? Where do you turn for advice? Who's experience do you rely on? I've been on industry bulletin boards where the advice is rarely consistent. As a franchisee, I can take the operations manual off the shelf, open it to "Complaint Handling," and get a step-by-step outline of how to handle the complaint. And if it sounds serious or they say they're going to sue me, I can call the head office and talk with someone who does nothing but help franchisees deal with complaints."

According to Woody, about 80 percent of construction litigation involves the roof. "Therefore," he says, "I don't take shortcuts inspecting the roof. HVAC [heating, ventilation, and air conditioning] is the next biggie, and you have to take your time there, too. In Phoenix, we have a lot of all-electric homes that use heat pumps, which is a mixed blessing. If a heat pump has trouble, it's not very likely to kill anybody like a gas furnace will. On the other hand, heat pumps are complicated and have lots that can go wrong. And fixing them is expensive."

To protect your business from legal challenges, there are several steps you should take beyond delivering outstanding customer service. Two of those steps include making sure you have appropriate insurance to protect your business, and always working under a contract.

Insurance

The standard insurance most home inspectors carry is called errors and omissions (E&O) insurance, although general liability is another option to consider carrying. In an article in the *Communicator*, a publication of the Foundation of Real Estate Appraisers (FREA), the E&O insurance policy is described as "providing coverage for mistakes, errors, and omissions in an inspector's report." However, if an incident involving property damage or bodily injury occurs, E&O insurance will not cover you.

For instance, if an inspector knocks over an antique vase in the homeowner's living room (property damage) or actually injures the homeowner by dropping a hammer on her head while climbing down the attic stairs (bodily injury), general liability insurance is needed to cover your attorney costs, as well as any damages owed.

Both E&O and general liability insurance policies are available through most insurance companies. And some industry associations offer insurance policies to home inspectors with membership. FREA provides a general liability policy with additional coverage "for damages which might occur after the inspection." The additional coverage is designed to cover cases in which an item that the home inspector checked during the inspection malfunctions down the road, injuring the homeowner is some way.

By joining FREA, a home inspector can opt for one of three E&O packages that come with membership: $1 million in E&O coverage for $1,620 annually with a "Class A" membership; $500,000 in coverage for $1,480 annually with a "Class B" membership; or $300,000 in coverage for $1,385 annually with a "Class C" membership.

Get It in Writing

"From one home inspector to another, you're crazy if you work without a contract!" says Bob Mulloy, in his article "Anatomy of a Contract," which is available at www.all safehomeinspection.com. Mulloy, a successful home inspector in East Bridgewater, Massachusetts, says that "a well-drafted contract prevents misunderstandings and limits exposure to liability by clarifying in advance what the rights and obligations of the parties are." According to Mulloy, the best way to protect your business from legal claims is to work using a pre-inspection agreement and a written report.

Many home inspectors draft their own pre-inspection agreements by looking at what other home inspectors have done, and incorporating the elements that apply to their business. You may find that you can obtain sample contracts from your industry trade association. Before putting any agreement to use, you should have your lawyer look it over, as well as your insurance agent.

Mulloy, a former teacher of the business of home inspection at Northeastern University, and the editor-in-chief of *The Inspector*, a publication of ASHI's New England chapter, advises that there are a number of elements that should be standard in a pre-inspection agreement. In his article, "Anatomy of a Contract," Mulloy outlines these elements. See a summary of these elements in the sidebar, "Constructing Contracts," on page 42.

> **Beware!**
> Home inspectors should read and reread the fine print in any contract they draw up, as this is what the customer (or his attorney) will hold you to. Make sure you are providing everything you said you would.

Constructing Contracts

According to Bob Mulloy, editor-in-chief of *The Inspector*—a publication of the American Society of Home Inspectors' New England chapter—the following are elements that you should include in a home inspection contract:

- ❏ *Business heading.* Your business heading should be prominent at the top of the document.
- ❏ *"Building Inspection Contract" or "Pre-inspection Contract."* This should be centered near the top of the form and in caps.
- ❏ *"This contract supercedes all previous communications."* Also in caps, this phrase should fall under the contract title of the document.
- ❏ *Data section.* In a simple form, list the client's name, address of the property inspected, file number, date, and fee.
- ❏ *Scope.* Under this heading, your contract should explain to the client that you will perform a visual inspection of the above listed property, including an examination of the exterior, roof, mechanical systems, foundation, etc. Furthermore, you should state that a final written report representing a summation of your observation will be provided.
- ❏ *Service.* Under this heading, your contract should state what services are provided.
- ❏ *Standards of inspection.* If you adhere to the ASHI Standards of Practice, you should tell the consumer and list your certification number. The list of items to be observed and those to be excluded as written in the Standards should be identical in your contract and your report. If you depart from or exceed the Standards, then you should also tell the client.
- ❏ *Exclusions and limitations regarding the report.* Under this heading, your contract should list specific items to be excluded.
- ❏ *Exceptions.* Your contract should explain to the client that unforeseen circumstances or personal safety concerns might exclude certain items from inspection.
- ❏ *Confidentiality.* This heading and language helps to protect you from third-party liability and tells the client that you respect his or her rights.
- ❏ *Estimates.* As every buyer needs figures to make intelligent decisions, protective phrases are beneficial under this heading. If you provide "cost to cure" estimates, you should explain how they are derived.
- ❏ *Fees.* Under this heading, you should list your entire fee schedule for services and elected options. Fee changes should be by mutual agreement. The inclusion of a simple order form will help to distinguish which services are elected by the client or excluded.

Constructing Contracts, continued

- ❏ *Limit of liability.* The legality of attempting to limit your liability to the cost of the home inspection is debatable, but such language is used by many companies in spite of recent rulings.
- ❏ *Acknowledgment.* The contract should be signed and dated by both parties. You sign in your corporate capacity, and the client should both sign and print his signature.

Source: "Anatomy of a Contract," by Bob Mulloy. Reprinted with permission.

Ethics and Standards

Another form of protection against potential lawsuits is to develop and adhere to standards of practice or a code of ethics early on. These will provide your business with established guidelines at the outset. ASHI has drawn up a code of ethics for the home inspection industry. You can read ASHI's "Code of Ethics" in its entirety at www.ashi.org.

You should also inquire about the standards of practice and code of ethics used by other industry organizations or associations. Take the time to think about your own ethical business code and what kind of reputation you want to build within the industry and with your clientele—a sure step toward building a solid foundation for your business.

5

Nuts and
Bolts

Now that we've looked at the basics of putting together a good foundation for your business and assessing what your start-up costs will look like, let's get down to the nuts and bolts of the inspection process itself. In this chapter we will cover the elements that need to be included during an inspection, extra services that you can offer your clients, the basics of report writing, as well as pricing your inspection services.

It's Elementary

When asked what needs to be covered in a home inspection, Bob Mulloy, editor-in-chief of *The Inspector*, a publication of the American Society of Home Inspector's (ASHI) New England chapter, replies "everything from soup to nuts." According to Mulloy, "Clients are hiring you to be their expert representative on-site, for what is most likely the biggest purchase of their life. A home inspector is in the communication business, imparting knowledge to a client so that important decisions can be made based on fact. A client expects the home inspector to be a know-it-all, see-it-all Superman with x-ray vision. Unfortunately, in the world of business, a home inspector must use a contract that places limitations on the scope of the home inspection, to both help the client and to protect the home inspector from potential claims. Those items that need to be covered in a home inspection are itemized in the ASHI "Standards of Practice."

Mulloy explains that to adhere to ASHI's Standards of Practice, an inspection has to cover "an examination and report on the structural system, exterior system, roofing system, plumbing system, electrical system, heating system, central air conditioning system, and insulation and ventilation system." Service above and beyond these basics can be offered to clients for an additional fee. You can view an outline of a typical home inspection on Mulloy's web site, at www.allsafehomeinspection.com.

Sherlock Homes

A number of the individuals interviewed for this book talked about how important it is for the home inspector to play "detective" while going through the home inspection process. As Woody L., the franchisee in Glendale, Arizona, mentions, it's important to use all your senses as you enter a home and start your inspection—use your nose, especially when entering areas like the attic, basement, or closet spaces.

And what about "hidden" defects? According to Dan Friedman, a home inspector and lecturer, home inspectors must be more perceptive when they are in the field. Even though, of course, a home inspector is really not expected to have x-ray vision, attempting to come as close as possible will only help a home inspector perform the job better.

According to Friedman, home inspectors can be divided into two camps: the "ostrich camp," and the "investigative camp." Those in the ostrich camp take the view

Inspection Fundamentals

The generally agreed upon elements that home inspectors should check for, as set forth by the leading national professional associations (including the American Society of Home Inspectors and the National Association of Home Inspectors) are:

- *Structural components*: foundations, floors, walls, columns, ceilings, roofs
- *Exterior components*: siding, trim, flashings, doors, windows, decks, balconies, walkways, garage door operators
- *Roofing*: covering, gutters, downspouts, flashings, skylights, chimneys
- *Plumbing*: piping materials, fixtures, faucets, flow, leaks, cross connections, interior drain/waste/vent systems, water heating equipment, fuel storage and distribution, sump pumps
- *Electrical*: service entrance, main service panel, circuit conductors and over-current devices, fixtures, switches, receptacles, ground fault circuit interrupters
- *Heating*: equipment, operating and safety controls, heat distribution, chimneys, flues, vents
- *Air conditioning*: cooling and air handling equipment, operating controls, distribution systems
- *Interior*: walls, ceilings, floors, steps, balconies, railings, doors, windows
- *Insulation and ventilation*: attic, wall, floor and foundation areas, kitchen, bathroom, and laundry venting system

that if they can't see something, then they're not responsible for it. Home inspectors in the investigative camp believe they owe it to their clients to issue a warning if they find anything that might be a problem. Which camp would you rather belong to?

Stories from the Trenches

During one of Woody's inspections, there was a sewage ejection pump in the back of a crammed-full closet under the stairs. "When I first opened the closet door, I could smell a little sewage," he says. "Strong, but not overwhelming, just about like a real busy public restroom. Then I couldn't smell it any more. I turned the faucets on in the basement bathroom and let them run awhile. When I went back to the closet and opened the door, the smell was there again, but weaker. And this time I could not only hear the pump running, but I could distinctly hear the water running into the tank, like a fountain was hidden in back of the closet. I found two caps were missing from the tank. The owner said he thought that was the way it was supposed to smell, since it had been that way ever since he bought the house new."

Woody also shares a story of why the home inspector should always be safety conscious during an inspection. "A few months ago," he says, "I inspected a three- to four-year-old house with a big, beautiful pool in a huge, professionally landscaped backyard. On the ground around the pool were all these floodlights—not low voltage Malibu lights, but 120V floodlights—some of which were no more than a foot from the water. Imagine a kid climbing out of the pool and grabbing one of those light fixtures to pull himself out. There was also a floodlight behind the waterfall. A 15-foot coil of Romex wire was lying on the ground near the pump, with one end disappearing into the ground.

"I put my tester on it and it indicated no power, so my first thought was it hadn't been connected yet. A few minutes later, I was by the house about 50 feet away and noticed a light switch in an odd location. I couldn't figure out what it controlled. Then on a hunch, I flipped it on and went back out to the coiled Romex. Sure enough, my tester lit up. Someone had left live, exposed electrical wire coiled up a few feet from a swimming pool, and no ground fault circuit interrupter (GFCI) devices to be found!

"Well, I wrote it all up. My clients were from out of state, and their agent, a real good guy, shot a video of everything during the inspection. When the sellers got the information, they called the 'electrician' who had done it, and he told them everything was OK. The buyers' agent then called me back, a little frustrated, because I said it was a hazard. I double-checked all my reference books and even called the city building inspector. He went nuts when I described it. I called the electrician several times, but he never returned my calls. I gave all that information to my clients. I heard later they had the same electrician go out and 'do a few things to make them feel better.' I guess I did everything I could do."

> ### Bright Idea
> According to home inspector Woody L., in Glendale, Arizona, "If you find a significant defect, document it and then leave the area. Go back later in the inspection and see what else you find. For some reason, many defects are located close to each other. At the very least, you don't want to have someone say you wrote up a page on a $100 defect and totally missed the $1,000 one 3 feet away."

> ### Beware!
> Wet crawl spaces set just the right conditions for fungus that can destroy wood or leave it vulnerable to insects like termites.

Common Problems

In a recent survey by the American Society of Home Inspectors, the following items were listed as the most common sources of problems in homes:

- ○ Improper surface grading and drainage
- ○ Improper electrical wiring
- ○ Roof damage
- ○ Heating systems
- ○ Poor overall maintenance
- ○ Structurally related problems
- ○ Plumbing
- ○ Exteriors
- ○ Poor ventilation

Going Along on an Inspection

Woody graciously agreed to let us tag along on a typical day for him, beginning with his arrival at his client's property. Please note that this will be a brief tour, touching upon a few select areas and items, and in no way represents everything that a home inspector can or does check for—that would be a whole book in itself!

First, says Woody, "I always begin my inspection by arriving a little earlier than my clients. This way, I'll have a chance to scope out the house before they arrive." Woody also wants us to know that he always makes a point to park his car on the curb in front of the house, not the driveway, since he'll be checking it in the inspection process. He then crosses the street so he can see the house from a distance, making sure that the lines of the home look right. "So what's supposed to be parallel is parallel, and what's supposed to be horizontal is horizontal," he says.

"Just by stepping across the street, you can get a whole different perspective on what kind of condition the structure is in," he explains. "You can also see things like sways or dents in the roof." Woody then draws a diagram of the house and makes notes to himself as to where the different roof penetrations are, such as the plumbing stacks, ventilation, and exhaust vents.

By now his clients have arrived, so Woody begins his inspection by first introducing himself. He then climbs onto the roof. "That is, as long as it is a roof I can walk on," he stresses. Woody explains that you should think twice, for instance, about walking on a tile roof because you might just break a tile. Not a good way to start an inspection or create a good impression.

Roofing Revealed

Woody then looks at the condition of the roof, asking himself if it is soft. He also looks at the condition of the shingles. How many layers are there? Are there flaws or cracks in them? A lot of times, Woody explains, there will be manufacturer flaws or defects in the shingles.

Another important point is to be sure to walk carefully when examining a roof. Although it has never happened to him, Woody's heard some stories about home inspectors falling through roofs. Because of this, he says, some of these inspectors refuse to go onto a roof until they've inspected the attic. "This is probably a good idea," says Woody, "especially in colder climates."

After looking at roof penetrations, flashings, and valleys, Woody climbs down off the roof and gives his clients some idea of what state it's in, by showing them his notes and a diagram of the roof and where problems exist.

In Arizona, the air conditioner is often on the roof, so Woody opens that up and takes a look inside. "I look for condensation line problems," he says. "You should make sure that the water that comes off the cold coils is flowing out of the unit properly. Not out around a seam and down onto the roof, but going out through the condensation line. I also look at the compressor to see if there's a lot of oil around it to make sure it's not having problems. And I listen to the unit up close. I also look for mold inside the air handler part—the squirrel cage fan that actually moves the air around in the house. Sometimes you can see a lot of mold in those areas, and that can be a big concern. I've actually had sellers who were quite ill with respiratory problems because their heat pumps or air conditioners were full of mold."

Beware!

Inspect for proper ventilation in any home. Ventilation can mean the difference between a sound structure and a deteriorated one. Ventilation is also important when it comes to air quality inside the home.

Exterior Exam

Once off the roof, Woody goes around the exterior of the property, looking at the siding, especially if it's composition siding because there might be some dry rot problems or swelling or buckling. "I look for cracks along the foundation," he notes. "Even though you're not doing a test inspection, you look for things like termite tubes or other type of tests you might want to make a note of."

On the exterior, he notes the location of shut-off valves, electrical meters, electrical panels, water meters, walkways, and any outside features such as something that has a pump in it that is powered by electricity (to make sure there is GFCI protection). And depending on the age of the home, he says, make sure there is GFCI protection on the exterior receptacles.

"As far as tools that you use on the exterior, some guys use a screwdriver, but I prefer a scratch-all, which is almost like an ice pick. It's good for poking," Woody says. "Take your scratch-all and poke at the wood to make sure it's not soft—that it hasn't just been painted over, and be sure and tap on it to hear if it sounds solid or not."

Smart Tip

Tip...

If a home has a swimming pool, this should definitely be included in the inspection. Check for physical condition such as cracks and bulges, the mechanical condition if things like pumps and filters, and for safety features such as fences, diving board security, and electrical work. You'll want to make recommendations for safety features that are missing.

Stat Fact

For today's electrical standards, a 100-amp service is the minimum a home should have to provide adequate electrical power. Service may need to be increased if a homeowner plans to add electric heat or AC, according to www.handymanwire.com. Circuit breakers, the site says, have become the norm, not because they are inherently safer than fuses but because fuses could easily be replaced with higher-amperage fuses to avoid blow-out, without regard for the size of the wiring which is what determines the fuse size in the first place.

He makes a point to describe the foundation of the house, determining if it's slab, poured concrete, block, or wood. "I'll look at the brick," he says. "If you see various kind of cracks, it can mean various things. Almost every brick wall has some kind of cracks in it. Most of the time, you'll see some cracks along the mortar line in a stair-step pattern, which isn't such a big deal, but if you start seeing cracks through the bricks themselves or large diagonal cracks, those can be pretty serious issues. Also look up close to see that walls that are supposed to be vertical are vertical and not leaning or bowed out."

Quite often landscaping will be an issue, says Woody, with people planting bushes or trees too close to the house. "Here in Phoenix, we get people who plant palms really close to the house, and the long fronds hang out," he notes. "They look pretty, but they rub on the roof the whole time and then when you get up there, you see a semicircle of shingles that are worn away clear down to the wood underneath."

Amped Up

According to Woody, the routine for inspecting a house varies by climate. For example, most of the electrical panels in his home state of Arizona are outside the house. So the natural time for him to inspect them is when he's still outside. "In most other areas, they're inside either in a garage or a basement," he says.

"When looking through the panel, basically you're looking for anything that's out of the ordinary. You want to be able to describe what kind of electrical service they have, such as 125-amp service or 200-amp service. Do they have breakers? What do they look like? What do the wires look like? Do they have aluminum wiring? Aluminum wiring can oftentimes be a fire hazard if they're not maintained right. Look for any type of splices or do-it-yourself jobs. If so, you may want an electrician to come out and look at it."

Woody checks the plumbing to see if it's hooked up to the city water supply, and that there's a shut-off valve. "I don't personally test every shut-off valve because a lot of them will fail, and then the people who live in the house will be without water and be quite angry with me. So if it's a gate valve, I don't test it. I'll just make a note to the people that they might want to have it checked out by a plumber so he can replace it if it fails."

Still outside, Woody checks the swimming pool. "You have to look and inspect that there's a good fence around the swimming pool," he stresses. "When I inspect homes,

---

Helpful Hints for Inspection Day

Here are some helpful hints to get you off on the right foot when inspection day rolls around:

- ○ Be sure to set up the date, time, and length of the inspection with the buyers' real-estate agent.
- ○ Allow at least two to three hours for your inspection.
- ○ Make sure all the utilities (water, electric, and gas) will be turned on the day of your inspection.
- ○ Ask that the buyer be present for the inspection.
- ○ Let parties know that 24 hours' notice for cancellation is greatly appreciated.
- ○ Let parties know that payment will be due at the time of the inspection.

even in retirement neighborhoods, I tell them there should be a fence, because grownups fall in by accident, too, sometimes. Then, of course, they could say, 'Well, yeah, but we don't want to do that.' And I can say, 'That's fine. That's your decision.' But [at least] I said that there should be one. And I have a little note that I put in all my reports that reminds people that the number-one cause of death for kids in Arizona is accidental drowning. Hopefully, that will scare them enough to know that they should do that."

Woody checks the doors and exterior lighting and receptacles, making sure they operate correctly, then he goes into the garage. "I look to see if the garage door works right," he notes. "If it's an automatic door, it's supposed to reverse not only on impact, but the newer ones are supposed to have a light beam that goes across that trips it. I make sure it actually goes up and down like it's supposed to and doesn't hang up anywhere. I [also] look at the ceiling in the garage. Sometimes you'll see where there's been some damage that's been concealed while the garage door is up, so you need to make sure you look at the ceiling when the door is down, too."

Code not Required

Still looking at doors, Woody checks the one that goes from the garage into the living area to see if it's a fire-rated door. "If it's a cheap, hollow-core door, you'll want to point out that it won't hold up very long in case of a fire," he emphasizes. "That's an area where it's almost like doing a code inspection, so you want to avoid that. You can't come out and say, 'That door's against code.' You have to be able say, 'I would recommend that you put in a better door for your safety,' or something like that. There's also auto-close features on those garage doors so the door will actually close behind you. There are a couple reasons for that. Number one is fire and gas protection. If you leave the car running in the garage, you don't want to forget that it's running, go in and lie down for a nap, and have the house fill up with carbon monoxide."

One of Woody's pet peeves is the little cat doors that people will cut a hole for in the garage door, so the cat can go out and use the litter box in the garage. "That's not a good thing," he says, "because obviously, you're going to have a breach in the firewall. Make sure the walls in the garage don't have holes or penetrations that will allow fire to come into the house from outside."

Oftentimes, the attic hatch is in the garage. Woody makes sure there is a hatch lid, so if a

Smart Tip

Tip...

According to home inspector Dan Friedman, you should examine every failure by asking yourself: 1) What was missed? 2) How was it discovered? 3) How regretful are you that you missed it? and 4) What could you have done that might have led you to an accurate warning or prediction?

fire started there it wouldn't immediately proceed into the attic. "Eventually, any fire given enough time can usually find its way into the house, but the idea is to give the people enough time [to get out]," he notes.

Leaky Pipes

"Inside the house, you start turning on plumbing fixtures," says Woody. "I go to several bathrooms and turn on showers and tubs and faucets, flush toilets, and then leave the showers and the sinks running, while I go inspect some other part of the house. This is so you can get a chance to see if any leaks show up."

If there are bathrooms upstairs, he notes, make sure the fixtures run long enough so if there's a leak, you have a chance to see it down below. "If there's a Jacuzzi [style] tub, start that pump going. I've heard of home inspectors who have had those hoses actually pop right off the pumps and start spraying water out of the tub in a totally concealed area. So you need to run that long enough to give it a good test. Look underneath the sinks. Look at the shut-off valves and see what condition they are in. Most of the time I just look at them, and if there's corrosion on them, the [valves] might be ready to be replaced."

He also looks for water spots and other types of moisture damage. "I look around the tub, at caulking issues, previous leaks, and damage to the floor. Sometimes they'll pull up old vinyl and put down new, and it looks all nice and new and sparkly, but if you go in there and actually push around [it's a different story]. I've got a moisture meter that can actually detect moisture through vinyl and ceramic, and it will give me an idea if there's something that was hidden either intentionally or maybe not intentionally."

Woody advises physically getting down on your hands and knees and looking at the area around the toilet to see if there are any leaks or problems. "Put your knee up against the toilet and push on it to see if the toilet's actually secured to the floor," he stresses. "In older homes, where an owner has installed ceramic tiles, I would say that at least half, if not 75 percent [of the time], the owner never installed the toilet back securely."

Bathrooms are another place to check the receptacles and make sure they have ground fault protection. Check the lighting and exhaust fans, Woody advises. If the bathroom doesn't have any windows, it has to have an exhaust fan to get the steam and moisture out of the house; otherwise, it will start having mildew and other problems.

Down the Drain

From there, he typically goes into the kitchen. "Checking the kitchen is pretty straightforward," says Woody. "Again, water is the biggest enemy of the house. Make sure the dishwasher's hooked up right, so it's not going to be draining the discharge out of the garbage disposal. Also look inside the dishwasher just to see what kind of condition it's in. If it's got a lot of gunk built up inside of it, you'll usually hear about it. These are things that aren't really part of the home inspection so much, but it's part of what you do for your customer to help them have more satisfaction with the house.

An important thing to check on cabinets, especially in brand-new houses, is to make sure they're actually screwed to the wall," Woody says laughingly. "It sounds funny," he notes, "but a lot of times, they'll put the cabinets up within a day or so after the painters are there. And they kind of position them by sinking in a couple nails while they true up the cabinets before they actually screw them in, and sometimes they forget to screw them in. So then the homebuyer walks in and loads it up with their dishes, and Grandma's crystal goblet is the last thing to go in, and the whole thing comes down. Fortunately, I've only heard stories about that."

Attic Static

Check in the attic to see what kind of structure is there. Is it a rafter, or is it a truss system? "[On] one of the first inspections I did, I was walking along in this attic, hanging on to the various members of the trusses," recalls Woody. "I grabbed one and it came with me. About an 18-inch section of this truss member was just missing. I looked around for it and didn't see it anywhere, which basically tells you that the builder just left it out."

In the attic, you're looking for any places water is coming in, especially around the penetrations in the roof, Woody explains. "Generally speaking, most leaks come in through a hole that was put there intentionally, whether it was for a plumbing stack or exhaust stack, but it's a natural place for water to come in. A lot of houses in Arizona have evaporative coolers on them, which are filled with water all the time and can get out of whack so they overflow and have problems. So you have to look underneath them really well. You might have a brand-new evaporative cooler sitting on top of a totally rotten roof, because the old evaporative cooler was leaking so bad they replaced it to sell the house—but they didn't want to replace the roof. So that's one of the clues I look for if I see a brand-new evaporative cooler, depending on the age of the home."

You're also looking in the attic for any wiring problems. "If there's electrical wire scattered throughout the attic like a bunch of spaghetti, then you know the guy went to a demonstration and decided he's an electrician," Woody explains. "Also look at the ventilation, that the air can actually move through the attic and cool it. Look at the insulation, what it's made of and whether it's installed properly."

Beware!
According to Woody L., the home inspector in Glendale, Arizona: Within 6 feet of a defect, there usually is another defect.

Finishing Touches

Bedrooms, living rooms, and dining rooms are pretty straightforward, says Woody, with not a whole lot of things that can go wrong.

"I mentioned looking at the air conditioning, but also on a house that has a furnace, that will be a separate system," he notes. "You need to run that and see what the flame looks like. It should be a nice bright blue flame, not a flickering orange flame. ASHI's Standards of Practice don't require you to do a heat exchanger evaluation. [However], you need to try and get an idea if you can see a big crack in the heat exchanger or not. But if you see a lot of rust or a lot of soot, that indicates service is going to be required on it. So you can recommend [the homebuyers] get it looked at by an HVAC technician."

Potential Problems

Here's a rundown of common potential trouble spots, many of which Woody mentioned during the course of his home inspection process.

- *Air conditioning*: condensation line problems and mold
- *Attic*: leaks, poor ventilation, under-insulated
- *Basement*: water spots indicating chronic seepage
- *Bathrooms*: tile walls retaining moisture, toilet instability
- *Ceilings, floors, and walls*: moisture seepage, musty smell
- *Chimney and fireplace*: cracks and deterioration in brick and mortar, creosote buildup in flues
- *Decks, porches, patios*: debris caught between deck boards or underneath deck
- *Doors and windows*: rot or deterioration, incorrect alignment
- *Drainage*: wet crawl spaces and basements, drainage should be away from the home
- *Electrical systems*: amateur electrical jobs (wires everywhere)
- *Foundation*: cracks or shifts in the foundation
- *Garage*: failure to have fire-rated doors leading from garage to main house
- *Gutters and downspouts*: clogged with leaves
- *Heating system*: excess noise and vibration
- *Hot water system*: waterlogged tank
- *Insulation*: asbestos
- *Kitchen*: cabinets not secured properly to the walls
- *Landscaping*: bushes or trees planted too close to house

- *Plumbing*: old piping, deteriorated shut-off valves
- *Roof*: damaged shingles or improper flashing
- *Septic/sewer*: strong sewage smell indicating system is full
- *Siding*: swelling or buckling problems
- *Swimming pool/spa*: failure to have a fence around the pool
- *Waste disposal system*: hoses installed incorrectly

Realty Times (www.realtytimes.com), an online real-estate publication, advises that home inspectors never make repairs themselves on a home they are inspecting, in order to avoid a potential conflict of interest. There are also very real liability issues involved in attempting to fix something you find when on a home inspection. The home inspector's job is to stay focused on performing an objective assessment of the home's condition and reporting their findings to the client.

Service Above and Beyond

The *Realty Times* notes that in addition to examining all of the main areas of a property, it is up to the home inspector to address "health and safety concerns, adverse conditions, and required resale corrections. Issues can be anything from minor roof repairs or improper venting causing carbon monoxide emission or a fire hazard to a defective light switch or structural failure. Sometimes issues suggest maintenance; some require repair; all are health and safety issues that a buyer wants to know about."

In addition to the standard elements that should be included in the home inspection, you may choose to provide your clients with additional services. What are these additional services? They may include testing for air quality analysis, asbestos, electromagnetic radiation, lead, pest inspection, radon gas, underground tanks, water purity, water penetration/damage, or well-water testing.

If you think you want to offer specialized services, you will first need to do market research in your area to determine what demand, if any, exists for specialized services of the type we have mentioned. You will also need to assess what the added start-up costs will be for any equipment required to perform these services.

Radon Rundown

Radon is a radioactive gas that can leak into a home from the ground. According to the Environmental Protection Agency (EPA), it "comes from the natural (radioactive) breakdown of uranium in soil, rock, and water, and gets into the air you breathe." The EPA (www.epa.gov) also reports that radon "moves up through the ground and into a home through cracks and other holes in the foundation." It can also enter a home through nearby well water. And here's the scary part: It's one of the leading causes of lung cancer. Old or new houses can have a radon problem.

Radon gas can be checked with special radon-testing devices. There are two types of devices, passive and active. The passive devices include charcoal canisters, alpha-track detectors, and charcoal liquid scintillation devices, and are available from your local hardware store. There are also active radon-testing

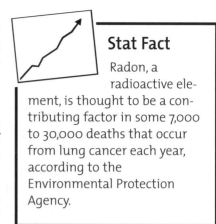

Stat Fact

Radon, a radioactive element, is thought to be a contributing factor in some 7,000 to 30,000 deaths that occur from lung cancer each year, according to the Environmental Protection Agency.

devices, such as continuous radon monitors and continuous working level monitors. They're called active because they require power to function, and should be operated by trained testers. Many of these devices provide a report of the data collected, which can reveal any unusual or abnormal swings in the radon level during the test period.

For more information on radon and radon-testing devices, check with the EPA's Radon Measurement Protocols, which provide technical information about the differences between these devices and which one is right for your inspection business, as well as how to obtain certification for professional radon testing. Radon-testing fees can cost the buyer or seller anywhere from $125 to $250, usually depending on the size of the home since a larger home will require more than one monitor. The EPA has produced a booklet called "Home Buyer's and Seller's Guide to Radon," which can be obtained from state radon offices or the EPA.

Reporting Your Findings

After a home inspection, the inspector informs the homeowner about the condition of the home by issuing a home inspection report. Some home inspectors use a checklist-style report, while others prefer the longer, more detailed narrative report. A great deal of thought should go into how you present your home inspection report, as your clients will be judging you by how well prepared it is. A home inspector's report should always detail what is being covered and why, right up front, to eliminate misunderstandings regarding what the inspection will or will not include. This is why it's also good to make sure the client signs a pre-inspection agreement (refer back to Chapter 4).

The Checklist Report

The checklist report is usually a pre-printed form the inspector can use to check off all systems examined during a home inspection. This report can vary from five to ten pages in length. Some inspectors may add a few written comments at the bottom to give supplementary information along with this form. Typically, checklist reports are given to the customer at the end of the home inspection. So if your goal is timeliness, this report style may meet your needs.

The Narrative Report

The narrative report takes more time to do than a checklist report, but its proponents say it provides the homeowner with more specific information, which makes a better overall impression. In addition, the narrative style may enhance your accuracy and reduce your risk of unintentional errors or omissions.

To get an idea of what a narrative report might look like, see pages 62 to 70. You'll find a portion of a narrative report provided by entrepreneur Frank J. in Carson City, Nevada. Frank generally includes a front page with his business contact information, as well as a table of contents, pictures, and notes at the end of the report on subjects such as ground fault circuit interrupters.

Typically a narrative report is typed and is around 20 to 30 pages in length. Its purpose is to give the potential homeowner or other client a clear understanding of the condition of the home. Information about the materials used in the construction of the home, conditions encountered, areas to monitor over time, maintenance issues, and how to troubleshoot problems should be included in a narrative report. Fortunately, there are many software programs available on the market today to help a home inspector generate a professional-looking narrative report.

Smart Tip

Tip...

According to the Small Business Administration, "The price of a service or item is based on three basic production costs: direct materials, labor, and overhead. After these costs are determined, a price is then selected that will be both profitable and competitive."

Mulloy, editor of *The Inspector*, describes the narrative report style as "a picture painted in words." According to Mulloy, "A narrative report is the best format for conveying knowledge and meaning to the reader with clarity of thought and little room for misunderstanding. The written word far exceeds a simple checklist when it comes to fulfilling a client's expectations and providing meaningful direction. Facts are recorded in a format that presents pure, objective, and unbiased evidence."

Fred B. and Brenda R., the home inspectors in Seattle, are also proponents of the narrative report. "The guy with the checklist writes a couple little words about a problem. If we need to write a paragraph or a page or two pages about a problem, we do so it's fully explained to the client so they'll understand the implications. You see a lot of times [home inspectors] getting sued because they might have said 'The crawl space is wet.' But they didn't explain the meaning of 'The crawl space is wet.' So the client didn't realize how big of an issue that was. We make sure they understand so we protect ourselves, but we also protect our client [because] they understand what the situation is."

Some inspectors go the extra mile and provide their customers with both styles of reports—checklist and narrative. Many say the checklist form is too short, with not enough information. And the narrative style is too long and involved for the client.

Robert W., the home inspector in Charlotte, North Carolina, uses a blend of the checklist and narrative forms. "What I use, I designed myself," he says. "It's just evolved over 14 years of doing it. We're licensed here in North Carolina, so we have to inspect what the state tells us to inspect. We have certain things and certain descriptions that you're supposed to make of things. For example, what type of roof it is, or what type of coverings are on the exterior. So I've got those things incorporated in a checklist. I use the checklist because it helps me do a better inspection. I'm reminded to look at something. I have to constantly go back and look at this or that, and the checklist helps me keep up with those things. When I find problems, I'll write a description out of what it is."

Delivery

Delivery of the report will depend on the home inspector's own style. However, it's important to remember that there is already a rigid timetable involved around the home purchasing process. So if extreme timeliness is your thing, you will probably want to opt for a portable computer and printer, and churn out your report for the clients right on the spot. But if you feel the report can wait a little while, you can go back to the comfort of your home or office, write it up, then mail it back, e-mail it, or take it by hand to the clients. Refer back to Chapter 3 for a discussion of home inspection reporting software.

The Follow-Up

Although it is not required, some home inspectors choose to offer a follow-up service for their clients. This often consists of a phone consultation, to make sure the homebuyer understands what went on during the procedure and understands everything on the inspection report. These phone consultations are usually offered "free of charge," as a service included with the inspection.

Bright Idea

Follow-up phone consultations provide the home inspector with valuable information about what homeowners are most concerned about. Keep a log of all your follow-up calls to find out what is at the top of the list, as far as things the clients were most concerned about. Once you've determined what they are, create or give some sort of tip sheet, booklet, or brochure to your clients, such as "Facts About Radon Gas" or "Cost Guide to Home Repairs," etc.

If you want to go that extra mile when it comes to preparing report information for your clients, there are other elements you can include, such as adding regular seasonal maintenance information to your home inspection report. This would include ideas on how a homeowner can best keep her house in great shape in spring and fall, or monthly and annually. You could also enclose any pre-printed literature from other sources that you think will be of particular interest or help for your client in the home buying process.

Pricing Your Services

In the United States, home inspections can run anywhere from $125 to $400, depending on what part of the country you are in. Many times, inspectors will break down their charges according to building type. For example, a condominium would cost less for an inspection than a detached home. Most inspectors also charge extra for special services such as radon testing, lead-paint testing, and well-water testing. Radon testing can range from $125 to $250. Lead-paint testing starts from $250. Well-water testing ranges anywhere from $100 to $300. The place to start in determining what your prices should be is to find out what the competition is charging in your area. You should also consider contacting any professional associations you belong to for assistance in determining competitive prices for your services.

Collecting Fees

Different from many other types of businesses, most home inspectors collect their fees at the time of the inspection. And there is a reason for this: They want to keep themselves out of the real-estate transaction process as much as possible, in addition to creating an objective profile in the mind of the client.

However, if you prefer to bill or want to wait until you have submitted your report to the client, it's perfectly acceptable to send a bill to the client's home address. Home inspector Darrell H., in Seattle, says he adds the words "Payable within 30 days" on his bills, to encourage timely payment.

Home Inspector's Narrative Report

ABC Home
Inspection Services
NV LIC #N-0000

John Jones
(775) 267-0000 Phone
(775) 267-0000 Fax

The following residence at 000 Mountain, Incline Village, NV, was inspected by ABC Home Inspection Services on May 31, 20xx, for the purpose of rendering an opinion to Brian Smith. While not technically exhaustive, this report is the unbiased opinion of the inspector, John Jones.

It is understood that the inspection was of readily accessible areas of the house and is limited to visual observations of apparent condition existing at the time of the inspection only. See INSPECTION AGREEMENT for other limitations. If INSPECTION AGREEMENT is unsigned, delivery and payment for the inspection report shall constitute acceptance of all terms on INSPECTION AGREEMENT.

Where available, photographs have been provided to substantiate findings. Not all areas of concern were documented with photographs.

❏ The house was occupied at the time of inspection, therefore limiting the inspection.

❏ The alarm system was activated upon the inspector's arrival. The inspector turned the alarm system back on upon his departure.

❏ The weather at the time of the inspection was approximately 75 degrees and sunny.

Inspection agreement signature obtained from client representative

(Original inspection agreement on file)

Home Inspector's Narrative Report, continued

❏ **HOUSE POSITION & DRAINAGE OBSERVATIONS.** For the purpose of this report, the house is considered to be facing approximately east. The lot was sloped toward the house in the rear and away from the house in the front, and appeared to provide adequate drainage.

❏ **WALKWAY & DRIVEWAY OBSERVATIONS.** The asphalt driveway and walkway appeared in good condition with normally occurring settling and cracking. The driveway area will require periodic, ongoing maintenance.

❏ **SIDING & TRIM OBSERVATIONS.** Where visible, the exterior siding, consisting of cedar lap material on the front and sides and T 1/11 material on the rear appeared in good condition, with an area of siding in the rear that was cracked and slightly shrunken. This is easily repaired. It was evident that the handrail for the front decking area had at one time been attached to the siding and had been moved. (See Decking Observations.) The finish on the siding appeared to have been recently refinished.

All visible trim areas appeared in good condition as well. All siding and trim areas will require routine ongoing maintenance due to the extreme weather conditions, which may sometimes exist.

❏ **DECKING & PORCH AREAS OBSERVATIONS.** The front entry porch appeared in good condition with no apparent concerns. The steps had the proper riser/tread ratio, with the steps having normally occurring weathering and cracking.

The front and lower rear decking areas, where visible, appeared in good condition with no apparent concerns, with the exception of the handrailings, which were noted to be loose. As stated earlier, it was evident that the handrailings on the front decking were at one time attached to the siding in this area and had been repositioned. The bottom posts on the rear decking handrailing were noted to have earth-to-wood contact.

The upper decking area, off of the master bedroom, was noted to be in need of securement, as it was loose and was easily moved. Further evaluation by a licensed contractor is recommended. The handrailings were noted to have improper baluster spacing. See additional information in comment section.

All decking areas will require routine maintenance due to the extreme weather conditions, which may sometimes exist.

❏ **GARAGE OBSERVATIONS.** The double-car attached garage, where visible, appeared in good condition with proper fire stops in place. The concrete slab, where visible, appeared in good condition with normally occurring settling and cracking.

The automatic overhead door operated as necessary with all safety stops in place. The entryway landing from the garage into the living area appeared in good condition.

❏ **ROOFING OBSERVATIONS.** The roof was inspected from ground level using binoculars. The metal roofing material appeared in good condition with some normally occurring snow damage. All fastening screws appeared intact. The fastening screws may require periodic tightening and replacement.

All flashing areas were intact with no apparent concerns. No leakage was noted at the time of inspection.

❏ **STRUCTURE OBSERVATIONS.** The poured concrete foundation, where visible, appeared to be properly constructed and in good condition with some imperfections in the concrete and some exposed foundation ties, which is only a cosmetic concern.

The crawl space beneath the house, accessible through a hatch in the garage, appeared in good condition with no apparent concerns. All visible floor joist and framing components appeared properly constructed and in good condition. The foundation vents appeared to provide adequate ventilation. The addition of a moisture barrier in the crawl space beneath the house would be advantageous to help alleviate any moisture concerns. This can be achieved by the use of plastic material, such as 6-10 mil visquine.

The type of roofing system present does not have an accessible attic space, with the exception of the area above the garage, which was accessible through a hatch at the top of the landing in the garage. All visible framing components appeared properly constructed and in good condition. The gable and soffit vents appeared to provide adequate ventilation.

No termites or other wood-boring insects were noted to be present. Further evaluation by a licensed pest control specialist is recommended.

❏ **INSULATION OBSERVATIONS.** While the type of roofing system does not have an accessible attic space, it is presumed that the proper air gaps and insulation are in place. The accessible attic space above the garage area was noted to be insulated with batt type insulation having an insulation value of R-19.

The crawl space beneath the house was insulated with batt type insulation, with an insulation value of R-19, some of which has fallen down and is in need of resecurement. This is easily done.

While not visible, it is presumed that the exterior walls are properly insulated.

❑ **ELECTRICAL OBSERVATIONS.** The main electrical panel, located on the exterior near the garage, rated at 100 amps maximum and appeared in good condition with no apparent concerns. An additional panel, rated at 125 amps maximum, located in the laundry room, appeared in good condition with no apparent concerns.

As the house was occupied, not all electrical outlets were accessible. All accessible outlets were tested with no apparent concerns. All GFCIs tested as necessary. No GFCIs were noted on the front decking area.

All accessible light fixtures and ceiling fans operated as necessary with no apparent concerns.

Some exposed wiring, which appears to be low-voltage wires for the alarm system, were noted in the attic space above the garage area.

All accessible smoke detectors tested as necessary.

❑ **PLUMBING OBSERVATIONS.** Where visible, the plumbing supply lines were noted to be copper with no apparent leakage or other concerns. All kitchen, bath, and exterior fixtures were operated with no apparent flow or drainage concerns. The Jacuzzi-type tub was filled with water, and the pump was activated with no apparent concerns.

The visible waste piping was ABS plastic with no apparent leakage or other concerns.

The 75-gallon propane water heater, located in the utility room, appeared in good condition with no apparent concerns. These types of units typically have a life expectancy of 8 to 12 years. With this particular unit, according to documentation upon the unit, being approximately 8 years of age, it should be capable of providing several more years of service. While a seismic strap was noted, a more substantial strap can easily be added. The temperature pressure relief valve was properly plumbed to the exterior.

The water pressure, taken from the rear exterior spigot, at the time of inspection was noted to be approximately 30 PSI. A pressure reducer was noted beneath the house in the crawl space. The main water supply shut-off was located beneath the house near the crawl space access in the garage area. The sewer clean-out was not located.

The house is presently on a propane fuel system. A line for a future natural gas hookup was noted to be stubbed-out beneath the front entry steps.

While the evaluation of the automatic sprinkler system is beyond the scope of this inspection, the control valves and shut-off valve for the system were noted to be at the side of the house, with some leaking valves noted. The timer control box, located on the side of the house, was noted to be loose and in need of securement.

❏ **HEATING/COOLING OBSERVATIONS.** During the portion of the year when the heating system is not normally operating, the summer test procedure is used. This is done by turning up the thermostat. This will result in a partial test of the heating unit; however, the adequacy of the distribution system and amount of heat cannot be ascertained.

The forced-air, propane-fired heating system rated at 80,000 BTUs, located in the crawl space beneath the house, and appeared in good condition. The blue/orange burner flame indicated possible improper combustion. The unit was in need of minor cleaning. The venting appeared in good condition. These types of heating units typically have a life expectancy of 20 to 25 years. With this particular unit appearing to be original to the house, it should be capable of providing several more years of service. All accessible heat registers exhibited good heat distribution. Further evaluation by a licensed HVAC technician is recommended. Additional heating was supplied by a wood-stove insert. (See Woodstove Observations.)

❏ **INTERIOR OBSERVATIONS.** As stated earlier, the house was occupied, therefore limiting the inspection somewhat. All floor and wall areas, where visible, appeared in good condition with normal wear and settling. The interior stairs had the proper riser/tread ratio. The handrailing appeared to be intact and properly secured.

The kitchen cabinetry and countertops, where visible, appeared in good condition with normal wear. All cabinet drawers and doors operated as necessary with all hardware intact. The countertop, where visible, appeared in good condition with no apparent concerns.

The bathroom vanities appeared in good condition as well.

❏ **DOORS, WINDOWS & TRIM OBSERVATIONS.** The interior and exterior doors functioned as necessary with all hardware intact.

The aluminum dual-pane sliding and fixed windows functioned as necessary with all hardware intact. While the thermal seals all appeared intact, several windows had what appeared to be exterior stain, which had dripped upon them. Some condensation stains were noted on several interior windowsills.

❏ **WOOD STOVE & CHIMNEY OBSERVATIONS.** A wood-stove insert was noted in the living room area. It was not evaluated for code or efficiency. The visible chimney and hearth areas appeared in good condition. (Before using, cleaning and inspection by a qualified chimney sweep is recommended.)

❏ **APPLIANCES OBSERVATIONS.** The propane gas range/oven burners were allowed to heat momentarily with no apparent concerns. The burners are not tested for accuracy. The self-clean cycle is not evaluated. The dishwasher was run through a cycle with no apparent leakage or other concerns. The waste disposal was tested with no abnormal noises. The grinding efficiency is not tested. The range vent fan/light operated properly. The trash compactor was activated with no apparent concerns.

The laundry area located in the utility was equipped with 220 volts, as well as natural gas for dryer operation. The dryer was properly vented to the exterior.

The attached inspection report was prepared following ASHI and the State of Nevada Guidelines. A copy of the guidelines is available upon request. As stated earlier, this report is intended to be the unbiased opinion of the inspector. ABC Home Inspection Services neither accepts nor assumes any liability for any latent concerns, which may arise in the future.

ABC Home Inspection Services appreciates your business. Please feel free to call with any comments or questions.

Thank you,

John Jones

ABC Home Inspection Services

Home Inspector's Narrative Report, continued

Summary

❏ **House Position & Drainage:**
Facing east
Apparent adequate drainage

❏ **Walkways & Driveways:**
No significant concerns
Normally occurring settling and cracking

❏ **Siding & Trim:**
Cracked area
Siding and trim areas will require ongoing maintenance

❏ **Decking & Porch:**
Loose decking support
Loose handrailings
Earth-to-wood contact on handrail
Normally occurring weathering
Baluster spacing
Will require ongoing maintenance

❏ **Garage:**
No significant concerns

❏ **Roofing:**
No significant concerns
Normally occurring snow damage

❏ **Structure:**
Imperfections in foundation area (cosmetic)
Exposed foundation ties (cosmetic)
Moisture barrier

❏ **Insulation:**
Fallen insulation

Home Inspector's Narrative Report, continued

❏ **Electrical:**
GFCIs in decking area
Exposed wiring (low voltage)

❏ **Plumbing:**
Seismic strap-water heater (upgrade)
Pressure reducer beneath house
Main water shut-off beneath house
Sewer clean-out not noted
Stub for natural gas
Sprinkler valves leaking
Timer control box loose

❏ **Heating:**
Summer test procedure
Blue/orange burner flame
Minor cleaning

❏ **Interior:**
No significant concerns

❏ **Doors, Windows & Trim:**
Condensation stains on windowsills
Exterior stain on windows

❏ **Wood Stove & Chimney:**
No significant concerns

❏ **Appliances:**
No significant concerns

OVERALL RATING
❏ Below Average   ❏ Average   ❏ Above Average

Home Inspector's Narrative Report, continued

Comments: The above rating was given due to the age and condition of the structure at the time of inspection. Where recommended, further evaluation should be performed to help substantiate findings.

While code at the time the house was constructed, the spacing of the balusters on the stair and decking railings do not meet the minimum codes of today's standards. While this does not imply you are obligated to bring it up to current codes, it would be advantageous to make corrections while making any future repairs to the railings as it would be relatively easy and inexpensive at that time.

PLEASE REMEMBER: Our service is established to help you identify and document most of the conditions of the property. This report is not intended to be an "ALL INCLUSIVE" list of every condition, but rather, to identify any major concerns that were visible at the time of inspection. Cosmetic items are subjective and normally beyond the scope of this inspection.

Upgrading Your
Expertise

Just as upgrades can make a homeowner's property more valuable, the same can be said for the home inspection service owner who seeks to continually upgrade his knowledge. The more professional enhancement a home inspection service owner can obtain, not to mention hands-on experience in a field like construction or renovation, the better—

particularly in this field, with its very real threat of lawsuits due to negligence. Let's take a look at some of the different educational outlets a home inspection service owner can plug into.

Train, Don't Strain

Don't underestimate the value of a good training program. No matter how long you've been in the business, from a few days to a few years to a few decades, home inspection training programs can provide the basics you need. They can also provide refresher courses or seminars to keep you current in this highly competitive industry. And don't forget about continuing education for your employees if you choose to hire additional help.

Some training institutes offer it all, including an overview of starting a home inspection business, report-writing options, marketing and advertising your business, and American Society of Home Inspector's (ASHI) required elements to be checked during the home inspection process itself. Others specialize: The U.S. Environmental Protection Agency (EPA) has designed special protocols for radon testing, as well as lead-paint testing. There are a number of schools offering certification for this type of testing. For more information, you can contact the EPA at www.epa.gov, or the National Radon Safety Board at www.nrsb.org.

Compare, Compare

Do your homework as far as learning what each training school or program is offering. According to ASHI, there are some schools that look and sound good, but fail to follow through on what they promise. In addition, their costs may be exorbitant compared to other schools offering the same format.

You also need to know if the course or the continuing educational requirements you're interested in have been accepted by the professional organization you are affiliated with, or want to be affiliated with. Asking experienced professionals in your area their opinions on a particular school and its course offerings could prove most helpful.

Smart Tip

Tip...

Before selecting a school, meet with the school administrator and instructors, if possible. Ask the administrator for telephone numbers of previous graduates so you can talk with them. In addition, talk with current students. You may also want to contact your state's school accrediting commission and ask if they have any complaints on file for the school you are interested in. You can also contact your state's Department of Education to see if any complaints have been lodged against the school.

Live and In Person

If you prefer learning in an atmosphere where there are live instructors to step you through what you're learning, there are many private training schools that do just that, either at their place of business or through continuing education courses held around the country.

The advantage of this type of educational opportunity over online or correspondence study is that you have immediate interaction with a well-versed, seasoned instructor. There's also the opportunity to exchange information with other home inspectors when you attend a course in person. Many inspectors say they like attending these courses because of the opportunity to network with others in the business.

Some training programs are designed for persons interested in entering the home inspection business. Some target home inspectors who want to improve their home inspection skills. There is even a school that offers programs where individuals from related fields, such as real-estate agents, appraisers, mortgage lenders, and attorneys, can become more familiar with the home inspection process.

You can attend training schools for varying lengths of time, from a few days to a few weeks. Classes may be offered on a variety of topics, such as technical training, business building, and sales and marketing. Several schools offer specialized courses such as commercial inspection, pool and spa inspection, and mobile home inspection. Many offer field courses in which students actually perform home inspections as a training exercise.

One private occupational school offers a 48-hour course held during six consecutive days in the school's training center. The program emphasizes the business side of home inspection with classes held on the art of customer relations, report writing, legal issues, business development, and the role of building code in home inspection. The graduates are automatically enrolled in the school's certification program. Courses are usually offered every two to three weeks throughout the year, and they provide refresher courses available at various locations throughout the country.

Home Study

Home study courses (sometimes referred to as correspondence courses or distance education) can have several advantages. Compared to a private training school, they are relatively inexpensive, and you can study in the privacy of your own home at your own pace without the distraction of other students. However, if you know that self-discipline is not your strongest suit, especially when it comes to study time, then a home-study course might not be your best bet.

There are a variety of home study courses on the market today. Carson Dunlop & Associates Limited, a Canadian company, offers a home study program. It includes a 10-week correspondence home course, containing 4,500 pages of text and 17 hours of video; Report Writing: The Home Reference Book, which details the report-writing process; and Clip Art: The Illustrated Home, a CD-ROM and book that contains over 1,500 illustrations that home inspectors can use in reports and promotional activities. They also provide technical support via the internet and a toll-free phone line.

In addition, Carson Dunlop, in conjunction with ASHI, has developed a home training system called the ASHI@Home Training System. This system contains 10 modules, each of which features between 250 and 500 pages of course text and up to 250 illustrations. To help students

> ## Smart Tip
> ### Tip...
> You and only you are responsible for your level of training. Do you feel able to go out and inspect homes after a few days of training, a week, two weeks? Always monitor your confidence level. If you're not feeling very confident about a certain aspect of home inspecting, set a goal for yourself to obtain training in that area.

work their way through the material, it is broken down into "Study Sessions," with time estimates given for the completion of each session. They also offer 6, 8, and 12-day courses as well as, new in 2007, 2-day, 3-day, or weekend courses. All students who successfully complete the 10-module training program receive a certificate. Check out their web site at www.hominspectiontraining.net.

Online Training

Distance-learning has become popular and more reliable with the increased expansion and use of the internet. Now you can take courses online in a variety of topics, including home inspection. For instance, the National Institute of Building Inspectors (NIBI) now offers web-based home inspection training (visit www.nibi.com for more information). Through their online courses, you can prepare for becoming a home inspector and stay current once you've started your business. If you prefer the convenience of online training, start surfing the internet to see what other course offerings you can find.

Keep in mind that online learning is not for everyone. You may have a good idea about how you would respond to online learning; if you have employees that you are eager to have ongoing training, you may want to give them options of either online learning, home study, or traditional in-classroom courses. Everyone learns differently and since the underlying motive is to be trained, you need to choose the right kind of training for you and/or your employees to increase their knowledge.

Course Pricing

Pricing for courses, whether at a training school or through seminars and home study, can fluctuate. For example, several training schools offer 11-day courses for

Beware!

Due to the proliferation of training schools and independent home inspectors offering different forms of instruction for the home inspection industry, prices can run the gamut. Be sure to visit many different web sites. And compare all costs, at all costs! But also compare the training itself and get as much personal feedback as you can from people who have actually done the training you are considering.

anywhere from $2,000 to $3,000. Many times, this includes the cost of class materials and professional certification. And some home study programs offer videos for anywhere from $30 to $60, depending on the length of the tape. There's also a proliferation of online courses offered on the web that vary greatly in scope and in price.

You need to take your time and select the program or course that best suits your needs and budget. Don't forget to factor in the value of the course in terms of whether it meets the standards of your professional association or certifying organization. Research costs and course offerings on the internet, through any professional organizations you belong to, by networking with others you know in your field who have taken courses, and by requesting written materials directly from the training companies themselves.

Why Train?

In addition to technical courses, there are other options for home inspection service owners to put them heads above the competition. Adjunct courses, such as ones on improving communication skills, management practices, or report writing will enhance an inspector's skills. Familiarity with real-estate practices and legal and marketing issues can also enhance your business. The more education you get, the more knowledgeable and polished you will appear to others. Ask yourself, if you were a prospective client, who would you want to go with? The home inspection service owner who has limited or "just the basics" education and knowledge of the industry, who replies to client questions through opinion and conjecture only? Or the well-informed, well-connected, home inspector with many classes behind him to add to his tool belt?

Another good reason for any home inspector to consider some form of educational enrichment is that you will need to pass the licensing and regulation requirements set forth by your state. As we mentioned in Chapter 4, there are now over 30 states that now have some form of regulation affecting the home inspection industry. For example, in Wisconsin, home inspectors must pass the National Home Inspector Examination and a two-part state exam.

The examination board developed the National Home Inspector Examination "to assist organizations and state governments to assess the basic knowledge and competence of practicing home inspectors. The test consists of 200 four-option multiple-choice questions covering 11 major content areas, such as structural components, exterior, roofing, plumbing, heating, cooling, electrical, insulation and ventilation, interiors, fireplaces and solid fuel-burning appliances, and professional practice." It costs $225 to take the test in most states that require it.

ASHI exams are available across the country and are administered electronically. The ASHI examination costs about $85 to take, and the organization advises examination candidates to read ASHI training manuals, in addition to books on construction, electrical wiring, roofing, air conditioning and heating, appliances, etc., in order to properly prepare for and pass the test. In addition, there are a variety of training programs aimed at helping you to prepare for licensing examinations.

Beware!
According to the Illinois Emergency Management Agency's Division of Nuclear Safety, that "any test lasting less than a week requires closed-house conditions. This means "keeping all windows closed, keeping doors closed except for normal entry and exit, and not operating fans or other machines which bring air in from the outside ..." See their web site www.state.il.us/iema/radon/radon.htm for more information.

Get Professional

Part of upgrading your expertise and your business is becoming a member of a national or local industry association. These organizations can be invaluable resources for the home inspection service owner, as well as a way to inform your clients that you adhere to the organization's stringent membership requirements. Be aware, though, that before you apply for full membership, some associations may require an assessment of your industry knowledge, especially before placing you in a training course or program. They may also want to review your reporting methods and any formal examinations you've taken. You may also have to provide documentation that you've completed a certain number of home inspections. Association fees vary and can run from $50 to $500.

ASHI has been around since 1976 and is considered the premiere organization for the home inspection service industry. ASHI's membership requirements specify a combination of experience, training, and fieldwork. Certification requires a number of qualification points, which are made up of education, experience, fieldwork, and a minimum number of fee-paid inspections and written reports, which meet ASHI's

Standards of Practice. ASHI also hosts the largest annual home inspection conference and expo.

The National Association of Home Inspectors (NAHI) is a nonprofit industry association, started in 1987. There are three levels of membership in NAHI, depending on the level of experience and completion of certain exams. An associate membership is available for those new to the home inspection field. The third level, Certified Real Estate Inspector (CREI), "is received only after an individual has conducted at least 250 inspections, passed the required examination, and met all requirements set forth by the Board of Directors."

To become a NIBI-certified inspector, you must complete an examination, trial inspections, and participate in training and continuing education. In addition, NIBI-certified inspectors must "successfully complete an extensive seminar that has a course curriculum covering the basics of all areas of residential structural and mechanical systems." NIBI also requires that NIBI-certified inspectors carry comprehensive errors and omissions and liability insurance.

Branching Out

Moving into relatively new but related areas, such as environmental services, can help upgrade your business, as well as serve as a source of extra income. Heightened awareness of environmental issues has more and more home inspection clients requesting such things as radon, asbestos, septic system, lead-paint, and indoor air-quality testing.

There are different regulations nationwide for the various forms of environmental testing, so if you are thinking about providing one of these services, you need to check your state's regulations and requirements. There should be a different and specific pre-inspection agreement for every additional inspection service a home inspector offers (i.e., radon testing, lead-paint testing, well-water flow evaluations, water-quality testing, termite inspections, on-site sewage system evaluations, etc.), and of course you should set a fee rate for each additional service you offer.

Expert Witness

If you're thinking about expanding your business by offering new or adjunct services, a seasoned home inspector could expand into mobile home, pool and spa, and commercial inspections. Or you could consider becoming an expert witness.

According to Able Home Inspection (www.ablehomeinspection.com/expertwit ness.html), an expert witness is often called in to help resolve "issues related to either faulty or negligent work provided by a contractor/tradesperson, or faulty or negligent services provided by a home inspector." Expert witnesses reportedly earn an hourly rate of between $100 and $200, plus travel expenses and any other expenses incurred.

Special Investigations

No, "special investigations" doesn't mean ghost-busting, although a client may ask you to find the source of a strange or persistent noise. When you advertise yourself as a special investigator for the home, a client could call you in for a variety of problems. They may want you to find the source of a noxious odor, or investigate why several members of their family are always getting sick during certain months of the year, or find out what's causing damage to a certain area of the home.

Because special investigations work is a relatively new offshoot of home inspection, there are as yet no additional regulations or licenses required to perform this work. Fees are highly subjective, and you may have to do some additional work to arrive at a fair price for the services you will perform for clients in your area. To protect yourself from liability, you should possess the appropriate training and experience to make informed determinations in any specialty areas you enter. Also, be prepared to talk about your qualifications, as many consumers will want to know your background and expertise.

Other Offshoots

The flexibility of the home inspection business affords you, the home inspector, a chance to branch out into other arenas or vocations you may be interested in. You might want to follow the lead of some of the home inspectors interviewed for this guide. Darrell H., the home inspector in Seattle, teaches home inspection at a local community college. Bob Mulloy, the home inspector in East Bridgewater, Massachusetts, writes newspaper and magazine articles on the home inspection industry and has developed his own narrative report writing system, which he sells on the internet. Other potential offshoots include real-estate appraisals, home repair, and home inspection training schools, to name a few.

Seven Tips for Success

1. *Remember to cross-train.* Strive to improve your oral and written communication, as well as your knowledge of real estate, financial, legal, management, business, computer, and marketing skills. Become knowledgeable about such specific areas as electrical, plumbing, heating and cooling systems; roofing and insulation; foundation and drainage structures; and interior components. That's right, a good home inspector's education never ends!

2. *Obtain errors and omissions insurance and liability insurance.* Even though you think you may never overlook something in a home inspection, the odds are against it. Be prepared.

3. *Presentation is everything.* Make sure your narrative report to the client is written clearly and concisely.

4. *Provide follow-up and consultation services for your clients.* This way, you can eliminate any misunderstandings by making yourself available to answer their questions regarding their home inspection.

5. *Take the time to give clients handy reference material about your service, such as a list of homeowner's FAQs.* These can include your qualifications, how long you have been in business, how many home inspections you or your firm have completed, the length of a typical inspection, how much you charge, your office hours and availability, whether you accept credit cards, when the client will receive their written report, and your professional references if you wish to include them.

6. *Design the best web site for your business that you possibly can.* Visit other informative web sites to get ideas, and to see what works and what doesn't. Don't hesitate to consult a professional web designer if you aren't comfortable taking on the task yourself.

7. *Add to your credibility in any and all ways possible.* Having a superlative title, such as Expert Witness or Commercial Inspector can instill confidence in your clients. Better yet, an official certification from a professional organization or association can add to your professional credibility, as well as arm you with the skills and confidence you'll need to excel in your chosen field.

7

Selling
Yourself

Make no bones about it, this is an important chapter. No matter how much money you have put into your business or how much education and on-the-job training you've received, if you can't sell a client on your business and your abilities, you might as well turn in your shingle.

Getting the Word Out

"It really takes a year, two, or three sometimes, to become established," says Don Crawford of National Association of Home Inspectors (NAHI), "because a new inspector is competing with the individuals who have already established contacts and leads and referrals. So a new inspector has to pour a lot of money into marketing and some advertising, [particularly] marketing their services and themselves to the real-estate industry, the attorneys, the lenders, as well as the general public. So it's a little bit of an uphill climb at first."

How do you find clients? Bob Mulloy, editor-in-chief of *The Inspector*, a publication of ASHI's New England chapter, says that the vast majority of his clients find him by referral from previous satisfied clients. "My theory is that everyone knows someone who is buying or selling a home," he says. "Do a good job, and they will pass your name along to friends and relatives. Truthfully, it has taken many years to establish a base of past clients and acquaintances but, once established, the resources grow exponentially. Initially, I knocked on many doors and distributed my brochures everywhere. In descending order, clients now find me by referral from past clients, other inspector referrals, the web, brokers, bankers, and the Yellow Pages."

Creating a Professional Image

Part of selling yourself is creating a professional public image. You should definitely plan to set aside money for the basics, such as corporate stationery, business cards, and brochures.

Fred B. and Brenda R., home inspectors in Seattle, did a number of special things to differentiate themselves from the run-of-the-mill inspectors. "We use a digital camera, and have a long, very clear narrative report. We also did a newsletter when we first got into the business, which we had delivered to all the realtors. We went out every Sunday for months, and would use that when we walked into an open house saying, 'We're the *Tiny Times* people, and we write this newsletter.'" See a sample issue of the *Tiny Times* newsletter on page 83.

Smart Tip

Tip...

According to the Small Business Administration, there are four aspects of marketing you should keep in mind—
The Four P's of Marketing:

1. *Product*. The item or service you sell.
2. *Price*. The amount you charge for your product or service.
3. *Promote*. The ways you inform your market as to who, what and where you are.
4. *Provide*. The channels you use to take the product to the customer.

Home Inspector's Newsletter

Front   Back

Beyond these basics, be aware that your vehicle can be an important image-maker. Keep it in good working order and consider the benefits of having your business advertised on your vehicle (be sure you have a business auto insurance policy if you advertise on your vehicle). Your business logo should be an integral part of the image you advertise to prospective customers. Use it on letterhead stationery, business cards, matching envelopes, four-color brochures, newsletters, sales materials, and reports. Be consistent in your design, and carry the logo and color schemes throughout all of your business printing.

Mulloy says the best marketing and advertising vehicle for his business is simply himself. "I do that by performing each and every inspection to the best of my ability," he says. "I spend the time on-site to gain the friendship and respect of each client. I go up; I go down. I get dirty. I go back and look again. I gather the facts, and I go the extra mile with a smile to satisfy my client's expectations by disclosing the true condition of the property.

"My next marketing tool is my report," says Mulloy. "I pride myself by documenting everything that was said and done, observed or not observed, in a narrative format that can easily be understood by my client. Through feedback, I often learn that my report was shown to friends and relatives with admiration. Remember the old saying 'telephone, telegraph, and write it on paper'? I guarantee that your telephone will ring if your report is accurate and impressive. Every client wants to get his or her money's worth, and a narrative report simply provides more bang for the buck."

Cross-Promotion

To cross-promote means to join with another business owner in an effort to attract more customers, so both of you will profit from the joint endeavor. Cross-promotions can include special offerings, such as joint mailings or joint appearances and events. You could think about writing some sort of brochure or resource book together. You could also offer discounts if your customers buy something from your cross-promotional partner, or hold a contest with the prizes being contributed by that business.

One of the payoffs of doing a cross promotion is just that—a payoff. With a partner, you can afford to participate in some of the more expensive marketing ventures you wouldn't even entertain on your own.

One of the rules of cross-promoting is to partner with companies reaching the same market. In the case of home inspectors, this would definitely mean realtors. The result could be something like a joint pamphlet or booklet explaining the ins and outs of home buying and selling, or co-hosting a local community or charity event together. You could also have a realtor distribute some sort of home repair kit with your company's name on it.

> **Bright Idea**
> Add your URL to business cards, letterhead, even your company vehicle if possible. This will heighten awareness of your online services.

Networking

Networking is also an important part of selling your services and gaining client referrals. Robert W., the home inspector in Charlotte, North Carolina, says that the little things you can do to network add up after a while. "What I've done in the past is go and talk to realtor groups," he says. "I would send them brochures and my price lists. I've [also] got some little scratchpads that I would take by the office and give to them."

Here are some tips for effective networking from Andrea Nierenberg, author and expert on creating and improving business relationships.

- Remember that first impressions count.
- Always make eye contact.
- Always do your best.

- Remember and repeat someone's name.
- Learn to ask for help if you need it.
- Be supportive.
- Never be late.
- Become an active listener.
- Always follow up.
- Set aside time to network daily.

Dynamite Direct Mail

Direct mail can be an exceptionally effective way to reach prospective customers, provided that you have done your market research. Once you know what target market you want to reach, you can ensure that your message reaches each recipient in a personalized way and at a moment they have chosen to consider your message.

Some of the home inspectors we interviewed said they targeted local realty companies in addition to buying mailing lists. It is often possible to purchase a mailing list that fits your specific target market by consulting a list broker.

Direct e-Mail

Consider doing an e-mail newsletter. This is a very inexpensive way to get your name in front of potential clients regularly. Your e-newsletter could include anything from tips to discount coupons, just keep it short and sweet and worth reading.

Collect e-mail addresses at every opportunity. Put a feature on your web site (see Web Power on page 86) that allows web site browsers to subscribe to your newsletter. Don't worry if subscribers aren't really potential customers but just read your e-newsletter for the valuable free information you provide—that's okay, don't forget they all have friends, relatives, neighbors, and co-workers who might be potential clients and to whom they might pass along your name and contact information.

Unlike regular mail where every newsletter that comes back to you is printing and postage wasted, it doesn't cost anything to send the e-newsletter. Collect names in a contact group in your e-mail software, create your e-newsletter, and push one button to get it to all the names in the group!

> **Tip...**
>
> **Smart Tip**
> Your growth as a business depends on how well you plan and budget your advertising program. Contact the Small Business Administration for information on how to set up your advertising program.

Web Power

It's the internet age, and you shouldn't underestimate the power of your presence on the web. Developing a web site for your business will not only enhance your overall advertising and marketing efforts, these days it needs to be a downright integral part of your marketing strategy.

Look at as many home inspection sites as you can. See which ones catch your eye. Ask yourself why you like a particular web site. Is it the eye-catching graphics? Or is it the quality of information that the owner has posted?

The Highlights

The following are some items to think about including to make your web site one that prospective clients will respond to:

- Don't include lots of large hi-quality images that make your site take a long time to load and navigate around.
- List your qualifications.
- Introduce your staff, if you have employees, and include their qualifications.
- Include a "Tips" section.
- Include testimonials from satisfied customers.
- Include a "Links" section to other great home inspection-related web sites and professional organizations.

Images

As mentioned in the list above, don't make your web site so graphics-heavy that it is time consuming to navigate around as users wait for images to download. People use the internet for expediency; they aren't going to wait around for the next page to come up, they'll exit out of your site and move on to someone else's.

You might decide to show images of inspection "finds" you have come across in your work (get permission from the owner—especially if the image is a recognizable location—who should be happy to grant it if they were happy with your work). A photo of a crumbling sill or other serious repair that a potential homebuyer wouldn't have noticed on his or her own is a great marketing tool to promote the value of your service. You could also show images of yourself climbing a ladder to a roof, walking into a basement—all exhibiting how you go the extra mile to service your customers. You could even show a spread from a finished report.

And don't forget photos of you and your employees! Knowing what you look like ahead of time can make customers feel more comfortable when they meet you out in the field.

Qualifications

Your education and experience are what is really going to sell your inspection service to potential customers. Be sure to include where you went to inspection school, any other work you have done in the inspections industry before starting your own business, any further education you've had along the way, how long you have been in business, and and specialization you have acquired.

Also list any organizations or associations of which you are a member.

Your Staff

Do the same as above for any employees who work for you, whether they are full time or part time. One thing about small service businesses is that customers often expect to get the owner of the business as their inspector. If you put your employees on your web site and make them a clear part of your business family, clients will already be familiar with them and not be surprised when it's not you who shows up at their prospective home to do the inspection.

Tips

Having an informational section such as a list of tips on your web site offers the prospective client "added value" as well as the opportunity to see that you know what you are talking about. Tips can include minor do-it-yourself household maintenance things like how to clean gutters or replace a window pane to more substantial information like how often to resurface a driveway to keep it in good repair or the importance of good drainage around a house.

You can indirectly self-promote by offering tips on how to be sure you are picking a good home inspector—and be sure your business abides by all your tips!

Testimonials

Ask satisfied customers to provide you with a quote to put on your web site. You don't have to put real or full names unless they are okay with that. Scatter them around the site in boxed sidebars that draw the site-user's attention. There is nothing like a satisfied customer to bring in business, so use testimonials everywhere!

Links

Visitors to web sites appreciate links to related web sites. You certainly wouldn't put links to other home inspection services, unless there is a colleague who does specialty work like pools or horse barns or potentially hazardous materials with whom you reciprocate promotion. Other sites might be informational for the customer, like links to environmental sites that explain why radon testing in your area is important. And you should have links to professional organizations and associations of which you are a member so that potential clients can check out their validity.

Products

If you sell products such as books or specific cleaning or repair supplies that you recommend, you will need to have a way to sell them using a shopping cart system and a web-friendly payment system.

Site Design

Once you know what you want to offer on your web site and have an idea of what you want it to look like, your next step will be to find someone to design your web site. You should ask for referrals from your business contacts, or conduct your own search for a firm that specializes in web-related services. Plan on spending in the range of several hundred to several thousand dollars for a professional web site designer, depending on how many features you want to include on your site. This is money well spent, however, since designers know how to maximize the return on your web site investment and provide you with a site that is manageable, interesting, appealing to customers, and professional looking.

Yellow Pages

Almost every entrepreneur we interviewed for this book said that an ad in their local Yellow Pages was one of the best things they did to advertise their business. Currently, a one-inch Yellow Pages display ad runs under $100 per month, depending on the directory and your location. Some inspectors feel this size is all they need, while others opt for a somewhat larger ad so that they can include details about their services or hours of operation. Display ads are generally priced by column width and depth in inches, and many directories sell standard sizes.

Special Promotions

A special promotion falls under the category of having your business's name associated with an event, or even hosting an event yourself, such as a charitable fund-raiser or a local athletic event. The goal is to get the name of your company in front of as many people as you can—in your target market—while staying within your budget limitations.

If you feel confident enough in your own knowledge of certain topics that fall within the realm of the home inspection business, offer to hold a free seminar on that topic. It could be for prospective homebuyers or sellers or for the real-estate community.

Web Site Success

How do you create an attractive web site that grabs readers' attention? Web site designer Jesse MacDougall (Fruition Web Systems, www.fruition.ws), offers the following five tips to stand out in the current crowd of over 122 million web sites:

1. *Brevity.* Web sites aren't read. They are scanned. Place the information that your customers will need to make their decision on your main page, in the places they will look. Be clear and direct about the services you provide.

2. *Learn about keywords.* A keyword is simply a word or phrase that a person would type into a search engine's search box to find your web site. Choose six keywords that best describe your services, products, and service area and use them in your site's main text, title, and menus.

3. *Professional design.* A professional business should have a professional web site. Visitors to your web site will form an opinion about your company less than a second after arriving. If your site is slow to load, or ugly, or poorly laid out, or unclear, your visitor will immediately notice and likely click back to their search results to keep shopping.

4. *Contact information.* The purpose of your web site is to help customers find your business. Don't bury your contact information deep within your web site. Place your address and other contact information on every page.

5. *Professional promotion.* Building a web site does not guarantee visitors; it must be promoted. If you are marketing your business to the local community, it may be enough for you to purchase ad space from local media outlets. If you would like to reach a larger market for your business, contact a web site marketing company who will make sure your site ranks well on search engines, finds the right markets, and is advertised efficiently and effectively. Beware scam artists—call any company and speak with them directly before you sign any contracts.

Hiring a Professional

If you're not interested in doing the work of advertising and marketing on your own, and money is no object, you could consider hiring a marketing consultant. A good marketing consultant should provide you with valuable information on building your business and creating a successful business through marketing. Some of the areas a marketing consultant may cover with you are:

- How to use promotions to maximize your results.

- Creating and maintaining a professional image.
- Assessing your strengths and weaknesses.
- Naming your business.
- How to make direct mail work for you.
- Pricing your services for profitability.
- Setting goals and achieving them.
- Understanding your competition.
- How to attract and keep clients.

Marketing consultant fees can run anywhere from $30 to $200 per hour, depending on the services you request and the size of the firm. Alternatively, you might consider hiring a small public relations firm to get your name out there.

Customer Service

The goodwill engendered through providing good customer service and establishing relationships with your clients goes a long way toward helping you establish a positive reputation in your community. Mulloy explains that once expectations are understood, bonding with a client should be a goal of the home inspector.

So how do you bond? Certainly being pleasant is a start. Smile and listen closely to what your client has to say. Remember that you are used to the home inspection process, but your clients probably are not—most people go through this process no more than two or three times in their entire lives. So try not to hurry through it. Take the time to explain to your client just exactly what it is you're doing and why.

Also, be sure to ask your clients if they have any questions. Mulloy suggests having the client take part in the inspection process by doing something as simple as "holding the flashlight" or "running the water while you monitor the pipes for leaks."

> **Tip...**
>
> **Smart Tip**
>
> Deciding what information to include on your web site depends on the target audience you want to reach and the image you want your company to project. Before meeting with a web site designer, make a checklist of what you think you want to include on your site and why.

Let's face it. You want to establish a rapport with your clients because they can be a tremendous source of referrals. Referrals ensure future business, and isn't staying in business your ultimate goal?

Managing
Employees
and Finances

Estimating your start-up costs, which we discussed in Chapter 3, is just the beginning of the financial figuring you will need to do to get your home inspection business started and to keep it running successfully. In this chapter, we will discuss the ongoing monthly expenses you will need to plan for, as well as what you can expect in terms of projected income. We will also address the basics of hiring employees, how to manage your finances, and how to find funding for your start-up.

Income and Operating Expenses

Many of the home inspectors interviewed for this book say the high-end income potential for this business runs into the six-figure category, with the right amount of hard work and dedication. Perhaps a more reasonable estimate of earnings potential, though, is the one that Mallory Anderson of the National Association of Home Inspectors projects. According to Anderson, you can expect to earn in the range of $40,000 to $90,000 after about three years, the period it takes to get your business off the ground.

The national average for a home inspection is around $330 per inspection and inspectors can expect to average around three inspections a week to start.. The home inspectors interviewed for this book said labor is always factored into the price of the home inspection, and their materials cost is usually only the cost of paper and printing. So what overhead costs will you have?

Bob Mulloy, an independent home inspector and teacher/writer in East Bridgewater, Massachusetts, estimates his monthly overhead runs him anywhere from $1,500 to $2,000. Ongoing expenses will include automobile operating costs (figure about $650 per month, based on a typical 20,000 miles per year, using your vehicle strictly for business purposes); telephone service; internet service provider; web site hosting; insurance (count on a prorated amount over 12 months); marketing and advertising; office supplies; postage; accounting fees, if you choose to outsource this task on a regular basis; employees, if you choose to hire them at the outset; and loan repayment, if you borrow to start your business.

If you choose to have a commercial office space, be sure to factor rent and utilities into your overhead costs. Depending where you live in the country, leasing an office space can run anywhere from $800 to $2,000 per month. We've provided a worksheet on page 97 to help you estimate your projected income and operating expenses.

Robert W. in Charlotte, North Carolina, rents a small commercial office, so he has monthly rent he has to figure into his overhead costs. "I've [also] got a couple different phone

> **Tip...**
>
> **Smart Tip**
>
> According to the Small Business Administration, once you have taken care of your building and equipment needs, you must still have enough money on hand to cover operating expenses for at least a year. These expenses include your salary as the owner and money to repay your loans.

and fax lines," he notes. "I've got internet access and a web page. There's gas expense and tools I have to buy. I [also] belong to an association, so I have to pay association fees. And we have continuing education in North Carolina that we are [required] to do. I have shirts with my [company's] name embroidered on it, so I have something other than a torn T-shirt to wear. I also have computer and software, copying, and fax machines [expenses]."

Employee Basics

Two of the inspectors interviewed for this book had employees who worked for them. One employed a home inspector apprentice; the other employed a secretary.

"I had a secretary for a long time," says Robert. "She went to work for another company about six to eight months ago, but she worked with me for almost ten years. She basically worked for me and another company at the same time, so I didn't have to pay for a full-time secretary. I was paying for part time and getting full-time results."

Now that his secretary is gone, Robert says he notices how much he had depended on her help. He also misses the fact that he doesn't have a live person answering the telephone. "The main thing that helped me was just having somebody there to answer the phone all day and take care of problems as they came up," he stresses. "The way it is right now, I have to wait until I get back in, or [customers] will just have to wait to get their problems solved. That's got me worried, because I keep getting busier. I will [be hiring] somebody to come in and handle those things because there's so many little things that come up during the day that need taking care of—a fax or a bill, or mail me this or mail me that."

These days the proliferation of cells phones can cover some of the concerns that Robert has. Keep in mind, though, that you don't want your cell phone on while you are on an inspection job. You need to keep your mind on the job you are on; interruptions like a phone call could easily make you miss something in your

Tip...

Smart Tip

It's up to you whether you want to offer benefits outside of wages. An employer is required to meet only Social Security, federal and state unemployment insurance, and workers' compensation requirements. However, to attract quality employees, you can think about offering either paid leave (including vacation and sick leave), insurance (including life, health, and disability), and retirement and savings plans. Other bonuses you may want to consider include reimbursement accounts, such as medical and dependent care, a company car, and performance-based bonuses.

inspection. And answering the phone while doing work for another customer doesn't make any customer feel very special.

So be sure your cell phone has a voice mail service. Once you're done with the inspection job, you can check your voice mails and return any calls that might mean future business. (If you insist on doing this while you are driving back to the office, be sure to get a hands-free attachment for your cell phone so you can talk and keep both hands on the wheel. Better yet, stop for a cup of coffee and sit in your vehicle in the parking lot and make your return calls.)

Smart Tip Tip...

Federal withholding taxes are required from new employers every month. As time passes, and if the business gets larger, you may have to pay semiweekly. Some large businesses pay taxes within 25 hours of each payroll; however, check with your state for payment rules.

Darrell H., the home inspector in Seattle, has one employee that he takes with him on every inspection. "This is an unusual approach in business," says Darrell, "however, two sets of trained eyes provide a slightly quicker and ultimately much more thorough building inspection for the same price. Many items such as chimneys are best seen from more than one angle at once, something a single inspector cannot do. Having the second person on the site almost completely eliminates the possibility of missing a critical problem."

If you are a home inspector with an employee or are thinking about adding one, wage levels should be determined by the degree of skill the job requires and how important the position is to your business. To find out what employees are being paid in the home inspection industry in general, contact ASHI or any other local home inspection associations. To find out what the going rate is in your area, contact your accountant. It may be worth your while to consider paying as much as you can afford to, particularly if you want to keep turnover low and eliminate the costs of having to train new employees over and over again.

Employee Payroll/Taxes

For the home inspector with employees, employment tax rules can be extremely complicated. That's why it can be a good idea to have a reliable outside firm handle your filings and payroll taxes. A firm that specializes in handling payroll for small businesses can charge from $35 to $40 per hour or more for their services.

As an employer, you must collect and withhold taxes from employees on almost every paycheck you issue. If you withhold too little from your employees' incomes, you can be penalized. The federal government also requires that you withhold your employees' share of federal Social Security and Medicare taxes. This is based on your company's balance, if any, in your state's unemployment insurance account. You will also need to hold out state income taxes, contribute to unemployment and workers' compensation systems, and match Social Security holdings.

Smart Tip

Tables for calculating federal withholding taxes are available from the IRS at (800) TAX-FORM.

Your employees will need to fill out a federal W-4 form and a Form I-9 from the Immigration and Naturalization Service. Some states require that employees fill out state filing forms. State withholding tables can be obtained from your state income tax department.

Keep in mind that employment tax rules change as the size of your company increases.

Answering Options

If you feel it is important in your business to have a human being answer customer calls, then an answering service might best suit your needs. Otherwise, you can decide between an answering machine or voice mail. If you can afford it, or if a family member volunteers to help in this area, have someone other than yourself answer your phones. It's always a nice touch to have a live person answering customer calls. It can also make your business appear a little larger or more established than perhaps it really is. Creating a professional impression is always important.

Outsourcing Options

As mentioned at the beginning of this chapter, the majority of the home inspectors we talked with said they would rather have someone else handle the financial end of their dealings. Most said they have an accountant to whom they hand over their paychecks at tax time.

Woody L., the home inspector in Glendale, Arizona, says that he hired a good accountant who has experience growing small businesses. He jokingly acknowledges that he leases every one of his employees, including himself and his wife. "I don't have time to learn how to keep all the government agencies happy and grow my business," he says. "I focus my efforts where they are most likely to produce a return, instead of trying to save a few bucks by doing it myself. When it's time to sell my business, I will have years of professionally prepared financials to back up my ridiculously high asking price."

There are also companies who offer scheduling and marketing support, all at a fee. The current ballpark range for this kind of telephone support is around $35 per scheduled inspection, typically with a stepped down scale after a certain number of scheduled jobs, so perhaps after 20 inspections, the price per inspection goes down a couple bucks. Voice mailbox options run about $25 per month. Billing themselves as a support service for the home inspector, they first gather information about your business in an effort to become familiar with your services, prices, market area, etc. They then develop a database for you, generating reports such as daily inspection orders, weekly calendar of scheduled orders, and messages received during each day. All reports are sent to the home inspector daily, via phone or e-mail. You forward your business phone to their scheduling center via your assigned toll-free number, and your phone is answered in your business name. They will also answer questions regarding your business.

Money Matters

What falls under financial management? Basically everything involved in running a home inspection business, including bookkeeping, record-keeping, taxes, and financial statements.

Bookkeeping

When it comes to keeping the books, many of the home inspectors we interviewed said they wanted to spend as little time on bookkeeping as possible, choosing to spend the majority of their time inspecting homes or thinking of new ways to build their businesses.

Unlike yesteryear, when everything had to be done by hand, home inspectors today have the convenience of computers and software. So if you don't want to hire an inhouse bookkeeper, there are many software packages available to help you get organized financially. See the discussion of accounting software in Chapter 3.

Record-Keeping for Profit

It is extremely important for business owners to keep up-to-date records. These records provide a financial history of your business and clue you in on how it's faring and the direction it's headed in. According to the Small Business Administration, records should be kept "to substantiate your tax returns under federal and state laws, including income tax and Social Security laws; your request for credit from vendors or a loan from a bank; and your claims about the business should you wish to sell it."

Estimating Your Operating Income/Expenses

Projected Monthly Income $ _____

Projected Monthly Expenses:

Phone service $ _____

Cellular phone service $ _____

Internet service provider $ _____

Web site hosting $ _____

Marketing/advertising $ _____

Transportation and vehicle maintenance $ _____

Insurance $ _____

Accounting fees $ _____

Office supplies/printing $ _____

Postage $ _____

Employee payroll and benefits $ _____

Loan repayment $ _____

Miscellaneous $ _____

If your business will not be homebased:

Rent $ _____

Utilities $ _____

Total Monthly Expenses $ _____

Projected Net Monthly Income $ _____

You can also opt to contract with a book-keeping business. In this case, you would drop off your receipts and sales slips for posting to a ledger the company keeps for your business. You are then provided with monthly statements and information for your yearly taxes. And if you have employees, many bookkeeping firms also specialize in handling payroll and taxes for employees.

Record-Keeping

You will need to keep accurate records. Without them, how will you know if your company is operating at a profit or a loss? If

Smart Tip

Tip...

Here are some general guidelines from the Small Business Administration for use in deciding what kinds of business records are necessary for you to keep. Ask yourself:
1) How will this record be used?
2) How important is this information likely to be?
3) Is the information available elsewhere in an equally accessible form?

you are taking business tax deductions, the law requires that you keep records for tax purposes. There are many tax breaks available for small businesses. Good record-keeping helps you take advantage of them. Small-business owners are frequently eligible for a vehicle expenses deduction. If you keep an accurate mileage log, the current mileage rate is 48.5 cents per mile against your taxes (this changes regularly so be sure to check the current year's tax information). Other tax breaks include the home office deduction. This varies from state to state, so check with your state office regarding home office income tax breaks.

Record-keeping forms include sales slips, customer accounts, and billing forms. Keep these documents on file, as well as forms that verify the date your business began and your fiscal calendar. These will be important in case of an IRS audit.

Financial Statements

Good financial statements will give you the information you need to assess how your business is doing. You should become familiar with the following types of financial statements:

- *Statement of financial need.* This is a form showing the total cash you have on hand, your total estimated expenses, and how much you will need to borrow over a certain amount of time.
- *Cash flow analysis.* This shows cash inflows and outflows over a period of time.
- *Balance sheet.* This is a record of the assets, liabilities, and equity of your business for a given period of time.
- *Profit and loss statement.* This statement shows your business over time and documents the amount earned, how it was spent, and whether a profit or loss

resulted. There are general accounting software packages on the market that can help you create monthly financial statements.

- *Income and expenses statement.* This is a type of financial statement that summarizes the revenues generated and the operating expenses incurred for a business during a set period of time.

Smart Tip Tip...

According to the Small Business Administration, a lender will ask you three questions: 1) How will you use the loan? 2) How much do you need to borrow? and 3) How will you repay the loan?

Funding Your Start-Up

Mallory Anderson, Executive Director of the National Association of Home Inspectors, Inc., says individuals should definitely have some cash reserve before ever getting into the business. In fact, he recommends keeping your current full-time job while building your home inspection business on a part-time basis until it is strong enough to support you.

Robert W. had a remodeling business first and kept that going while he slowly tested the waters in home inspection. "I was doing the remodeling business, and as inspections would come in, I would do them. As [the inspections] gradually picked up, I worked my way out of the remodeling business, and I eventually sold it to somebody. I worked for them for a year, and that helped get me more into home inspections full time."

If you find you will need financing for your home inspection venture, there are several ways to accomplish this. Some inspectors obtain a small-business loan if they lack capital, while others feel more confident borrowing the funds from relatives or friends.

If you choose to go through a bank for your loan, remember that small-business loan criteria vary from bank to bank, but all these lending institutions will want to see hard assets, such as property, motor vehicles, or equipment that can be used as collateral. They will also want to see your most recent tax returns, financial statements, and cash-flow projections, in addition to a well-thought-out business plan. A clear description of your experience and management capabilities, as well as the expertise of other key personnel will also be requested.

Beware!

Statistics show that the second leading reason why businesses fail is inadequate accounting procedures. Undercapitalization is the first.

Other lending institutions include commercial finance companies, local development companies, life insurance companies, and the Small Business Administration. Unfortunately, ven-

Funding Pointers

Before you decide on a strategy for funding your start-up, you should ask yourself the following questions:

1. How much available capital do you have to invest in starting your business?
2. How much money can you afford to lose?
3. Will you go into business by yourself or with partners? How much can your partner(s) invest?
4. Are any of your friends or family willing to invest in your company?
5. Do you have savings or additional income to live on while starting your business?
6. Will you need financing and, if so, how much and over what period of time?
7. What sources will you try to obtain financing from?

ture capital firms will probably not be a realistic option, since these firms generally focus on businesses with the potential for very high profits.

Then there are your relatives and friends. If any one of your friends or family is open to the idea of discussing a loan with you, here are a few helpful hints. Talk with them about your plans for your business venture as professionally as you can. Present the information just as you would if you were talking to a loan officer at the bank. Have your financial information (statements, tax returns, etc.) ready to show them. Also, prepare some sort of written loan agreement that you can both sign. This will eliminate any confusion as to the terms of the loan and help to keep your relationship harmonious. Always tell them if you are committing your own funds toward the financing of your business. Risking your own money gives others confidence when they invest their own capital in your business.

Smart Tip

Tip...

According to the Small Business Administration, you should prepare and understand two basic financial statements: 1) the balance sheet, which is a record of assets, liabilities, and capital; and 2) the income (profit and loss) statement, a summary of your earnings and expenses over a given period of time.

Inspection Lessons
Pass or Fail

In the previous chapters, we've provided you with the ins and outs of the home inspection business. Now that you've had an opportunity to find out what the industry involves, we're going to impart some insider advice from those in the know—the home inspection business owners we interviewed for this book. You'll find out what factors they think contribute to success and failure in the home inspection business.

Common Pitfalls

Fred B., the home inspector in Seattle, says that one common reason for failure in this business, or any for that matter, is lack of marketing. "It was, for us, a lot of work to get up and going," he says. "It took us seven months to get the first three inspections, and when you think of it, most work comes to a home inspector from a real-estate agent who gives out a list of referrals. There is no strong reason for a real-estate person to use someone who is new and untested, because the home inspector can make big problems. We have to do the work correctly. We have to be fair, honest, and unbiased, but for many real-estate agents, a new home inspector is an unknown commodity. So you need to be a self-promoter."

Some reasons for failure according to Woody L., the franchisee in Glendale, Arizona, are: "1) tradesmen getting into the business, thinking they know everything and finding out they know a lot about a new house, but nothing about a 40-year-old one; 2) home inspectors lying awake at night, feeling isolated, worrying, and letting emotions decide how they will run their business rather than logic and sound business principles (budgeting and planning take the mystery and fear out of running a business); [and] 3) poor training and little or no follow-up education—everything is constantly changing, and you have to keep up."

It's All About Perspective

A number of the inspectors interviewed for this book mentioned that in order to be successful, you need to be good at putting things in perspective for both the client and the realtor when reporting on the condition of a home after the inspection. Just what is meant by "perspective"? Scott Clements, former public relations director for the California Real Estate Inspectors Association, explained it this way: "The real-estate community has to have a great deal of trust that you can communicate your findings to your clientele and that you're able to articulate them in such a fashion that they clearly get the picture. Of course, they don't want the person to be scared off, so you can't exaggerate or make the conditions to be more than they are. You need to put them in perspective.

"For instance, if you're looking at a 35-year-old home with an original roof, and you indicate that the roof is aged, well, of course, that's obvious. But you need to be able to convey that to the client. You can't just get off the roof and say 'Oh, that roof is toast.' You need to put it in perspective. So being able to convey the information properly and put it in the right perspective is the most important way to get the confidence of the real-estate community," Clements advises.

Smart Tip

Tip...

The Small Business Administration has offices in nearly every major city in the country. They sponsor a variety of counseling, training, and information services including the Service Corps of Retired Executives, Business Information Centers, and Small Business Development Centers.

According to Robert W., the home inspector in North Carolina, if you don't know how to get along with the realtors, or you don't know how to get along with the buyers, that's a real problem. "Then on top of that, if you alarm the buyer with something that's not a big deal, you're going to alienate not only the buyer, but the realtor," he notes. "You can go in and do a good, honest inspection and the sale will fall through, and that's one of the things that happens. But you can't go in and say things like 'This is the worst house I've ever seen. I wouldn't buy this for nothing.' This is not why you're being paid. You're being paid to point out the defects. You don't offer opinions [such as] 'I hate the purple carpet.' I think a lot of guys fail because they're too strong in their opinions."

Experience Necessary

About half the home inspectors interviewed for this book said they felt it was necessary to have some sort of construction, engineering, or remodeling experience to be an effective home inspector. And all of them agreed that continuing education plays a vital role in helping an inspector be the best that they can be.

Fred B. cautions that home inspection is a high-liability business. Home inspectors are sued frequently because they either missed something or the client thought they missed something.

Bob Mulloy, the inspector in East Bridgewater, Massachusetts, attributes trying to establish a reputation for speed on the job, cheap rates, and a simple checklist report as why some inspectors fail to make it in the business. "Such home inspectors fail to gather all the facts, fail to accurately document the condition of the property, fail to transfer the true meaning of each observation to their client, and fail to stay out of court," he observes.

Recipe for Success

"In my opinion, for someone to succeed as a home inspector, he or she must be willing to listen, yet maintain control as the expert on-site," says Mulloy. "The successful home inspector establishes a methodology while on-site that follows an efficient pathway for complete investigation, fact-gathering, and recording of data. The successful inspector is both a salesman and an effective communicator who adheres to a code of ethics. He or she is respected as an inspector who is thorough, yet fair and discloses conditions with a bed-side manner that is informative, yet not alarming."

Here are Woody L.'s thoughts on what you need to become successful in the home inspection business:

Stat Fact

More than 2,700 chambers of commerce are located throughout the United States to provide assistance as you get your business underway.

- "willingness and discipline to consistently work harder than you ever have for less than you ever have while the business gets going;

- giving your family the time and attention they deserve so you can be truly happy when you work;

- then let that happiness, satisfaction, and work ethic show through to people you deal with. Success sells, and nothing shows success more than a genuine smile and a cheerful attitude."

Take the High Road

Robert W. says you have to be consistent and honest. In other words, he says, "If you find a piece of decayed wood, you have to tell everybody involved in that house where that piece of decayed wood is. You can't hide it. You have to be honest. But being honest also means telling people that you're not perfect. That you're not going to find 100 percent of everything that comes up. And you can miss something. You may miss something here and there, but in my opinion, if you're just honest in what you do and act like you're interested in doing the inspection instead of getting the money, I think you could be successful at it."

Take It Slowly

"Go slowly!" says Mulloy. "Take your time and do the research. Find a local chapter of ASHI [American Society of Home Inspectors] and attend one of their monthly meetings. See if the local members offer a 'tag-along' service and attend several home inspections. Sample the waters by observing a professional at work and decide if you like what you see. Attend educational seminars or annual meetings and learn what there is to learn. Check out your local colleges and see what educational opportunities are available. Check with the state authorities to see if a license is required and what qualifications are needed. Visit the ASHI Web site and obtain all materials of general interest or your desired area of study."

Clements advises all home inspectors to participate in professional associations as much as possible. "The best opportunity for an inspector is to learn from other experienced inspectors," he notes. On a national scope, Clements recommends getting involved with ASHI, and other state associations, too. "For instance, in California, there is CREIA. So there are national and state associations that allow inspectors to network with other inspectors. They also provide a great deal of educational opportunities. Both ASHI and CREIA put on annual conferences so inspectors can come and learn about the business from other inspectors and other experts in specified fields. [It's] an opportunity to bounce ideas and questions off [others] and learn techniques. I think the associations have the best advice for a brand-new [home] inspector."

Smart Tip

Tip...

In addition to offering regular home inspection courses, many home inspection training schools also offer classes in marketing and promotions. Consider it an investment toward your business' success.

A Service-Oriented Business

"[Home inspection] is definitely a service business," according to Fred B. and Brenda R., the business partners in Seattle. "There's the satisfaction of helping people. We don't like it when we have to help someone walk away from a home, but we like it when we're educating people—first-time homebuyers. They don't know a lot of the basic things about how to take care of a house. And it's nice [to educate them]. I was never a homeowner either until a few years ago, so I can appreciate what there is to learn. There [are] a lot of little tips, and a home inspector can do a lot of educating in a home inspection."

So there you have it. Yes, it does require a certain amount of expertise, as well as a strong work ethic and a commitment to continuing education to succeed in this field. Here's hoping that you, too, will develop the unbridled enthusiasm for the home inspection industry that the inspectors interviewed for this book possess. Good luck and happy inspecting!

Appendix
Home Inspection Resources

They say you can never be rich enough or young enough. While these could be argued, we believe, "You can never have enough resources." Therefore, we present for your consideration a wealth of sources for you to check into, check out, and harness for your own personal information blitz.

These sources are tidbits, ideas to get you started on your research. They are by no means the only sources out there, and they should not be taken as the Ultimate Answer. We have done our research, but businesses do tend to move, change, fold, and expand. As we have repeatedly stressed, do your homework. Get out and start investigating.

As an additional tidbit to get you going, we strongly suggest the following: If you haven't yet joined the internet age, do it! Surfing the net is like waltzing through a vast library, with a breathtaking array of resources literally at your fingertips.

Associations

American Society of Home Inspectors, Inc. (ASHI), 932 Lee St., #101, Des Plaines, IL 60016-6546, (800) 743-ASHI, www.ashi.com

California Real Estate Inspection Association (CREIA), 1445 N. Sunrise Way, Suite 101, Palm Springs, CA 92262, (800) 848-7342, www.creia.com

The Foundation of Real Estate Appraisers, 4907 Morena Blvd., #1415, San Diego, CA 92117, (800) 882-4410, www.frea.com

National Association of Home Inspectors (NAHI), 4248 Park Glen Rd., Minneapolis, MN 55416, (800) 448-3942, www.nahi.org

The National Association of Realtors, (800) 874-6500, www.realtor.org

National Institute of Building Inspectors (NIBI), 424 Vosseller Ave., Bound Brook, NJ 08805, (888) 281-6424, www.nibi.com

Books

The Complete Book of Home Inspection, by Norman Becker, Tab Books

The Home Reference Book, Carson Dunlop & Associates Limited, 120 Carlton St., #407, Toronto, ON M5A 4K2, www.carsondunlop.com

The Illustrated Home, Carson Dunlop & Associates Limited, 120 Carlton St., # 407, Toronto, ON M5A 4K2, www.carsondunlop.com

The Stanley Complete Revised Step-by-Step Book of Home Repair and Improvement, by James A. Hufnagel, Simon & Schuster

Start Your Own Home Inspection Business, Prentice Hall Press, Paramus, NJ 07652, www.phdirect.com

Uniform Building Code, ICBO, 5360 Workman Mill Rd., Whittier, CA 90601-2298, www.icbo.org

Conventions and Expos

Inspection Training Associates' Inspection Expo, 1050 Los Vallecitos Blvd., #109, San Marcos, CA 92069, (800) 323-9235, www.home-inspect.com

InspectionWorld Expo, American Society of Home Inspectors, 932 Lee St., #101, Des Plaines, IL 60016-6546, (800) 743-ASHI, www.ashi.org

Experts

Dan Friedman, home inspector and lecturer, see his article "Developing Your X-Ray Vision," at www.inspect-ny.com/ashi/x-ray.html

Bob Mulloy, ALLSAFE Home Inspection Service Inc., 102 N. Water St., East Bridgewater, MA 02333, (800) 636-7170, (508) 378-7170, www.allsafehomeinspection.com

Forms

InspectorStuff, 728 Front St., Ste. C, Louisville, CO 80027, (800) 490-6907, www.inspectorstuff.com

Franchises

AmeriSpec, 889 Ridge Lake Blvd., Memphis, TN 38120, (901) 597-8508, www.amerispecfranchise.com

Pillar to Post, 13902 Dale Mabry Hwy., #300, Tampa, FL 33618, (813) 962-4461, www.pillartopost.com

Government Agencies

Bureau of Labor Statistics, Division of Information Services, 2 Massachusetts Ave. NE, Rm. 2860, Washington, DC 20212, www.stats.bls.gov

Environmental Protection Agency, 1200 Pennsylvania Ave. NW, Washington, DC 20460, www.epa.gov

Small Business Administration, 409 Third St. SW, Washington, DC 20416, (202) 205-6533, www.sbaonline.sba.gov

U.S. Census Bureau, 4600 Silver Hill Rd., Washington, DC 20233, (301) 457-4608, www.census.gov

U.S. Consumer Product Safety Commission, Eastern Regional Ctr., 201 Vareck St., Rm. 903, New York, NY 10014-4811, (212) 620-4120, www.cpsc.gov

U.S. Department of Housing and Urban Development, 451 Seventh St. SW, Washington, DC 20410, (202) 708-1112, www.hud.gov

U.S. Department of the Interior, 1849 C St. NW, Washington, DC 20240, (202) 208-3100, www.doi.gov

U.S. Department of Labor, 200 Constitution Ave. NW, Washington, DC 20210, (866) 4-USA-DOL, www.dol.gov

▲

Home Study/Correspondence Courses

ASHI@HOME, Carson Dunlop & Associates Limited,120 Carlton St., #407, Toronto, ON M5A 4K2, (800) 268-7070, www.carsondunlop.com

Accu-spect Home Inspector Institute, 95 Keddy Blvd., Chicopee, MA 01020-3919, (800) 233-2758, www.javanet.com

Carson Dunlop Home Study System, Carson Dunlop & Associates Limited, 120 Carlton St., #407, Toronto, ON M5A 4K2, (800) 268-7070, www.carsondunlop.com

HE—School of Building Inspection, (888) 466-4677, www.hometraining.com

Radon Testing

Radalink Inc., 5599 Peachtree Rd., Atlanta, GA 30341-2309, (800) 295-4655, www.radalink.com

Radon Testing Corporation of America (RTCA), 2 Hayes St., Elmsford, NY 10523, (914) 345-3380, www.rtca.com

Reporting Software

DNA Reporting System, ALLSAFE Home Inspection Service Inc., (800) 636-7170, www.allsafehomeinspection.com

Home Inspection 2000, 8230 Collier Blvd., Naples, FL 34114, (239) 775-9820, www.homeinspection2000.com

HomePro Systems Inc., 2841 Hartland Rd., #201, Falls Church, VA 22043, (800) HOMEPRO, www.home-pro.com

Successful Home Inspection Service Owners

Camelot Home Inspections, Martin Hewitt, (805) 471-9447, www.homeinspectionser vices.com

SAFE & SOUND Home Inspections, Darrell Hay, (800) 798-7181, www.safesound home.com

Seattle Home Inspections Inc., Fred Bishop/Brenda Rosch, 4838 19th Ave. S., Seattle, WA 98108, (206) 768-2715

Tools

Inspection Tools Unlimited, 4722 N.W. Boca Raton Blvd., Ste. C-108, Boca Raton, FL 33431, (800) 226-6299, www.inspectioncentral.com

InspectorTools, 4848 Colt Street, #11, Ventura, CA 93003-7732, (800) 895-4916, www.inspectortools.com

Professional Equipment, 90 Plant Ave., #3, Hauppauge, NY 11788, (800) 334-9291, www.professionalequipment.com

Trade Publications

The ASHI Reporter, American Society of Home Inspectors, 932 Lee St., #101, Des Plaines, IL 60016-6546, (800) 743-ASHI, www.ashi.org

The Communicator Magazine, The Foundation of Real Estate Appraisers, 4907 Morena Blvd., #1415, San Diego, CA 92117, (800) 882-4410, www.frea.com

The Journal of Light Construction, 186 Allen Brook Ln., Williston, VT 05495, (802) 879-3335, www.jlconline.com

Realtor, National Association of Realtors, (800) 874-6500, www.nar.realtor.org

Training Schools

Allied Schools, 22952 Alcade Dr., Laguna Hills, CA 92653, (888) 925-2108, www.homeinspectioncourse.com

Home Inspection Institute of America, 314 Main St., Yalesville, CT 06492, (203) 284-2311, www.inspecthomes.com

Inspection Training Associates, 1050 Los Vellecitos Blvd., #109, San Marcos, CA 92069 (888) 323-9235, www.home-inspect.com

Glossary

Ampere: measurement term for electricity flow through a conductor; abbreviated "amp."

Caulking: material used to seal seams, cracks, or joints.

Checklist report: a short report form in which the home inspector can check off items examined during the home inspection.

Crawl space: an unfinished, partial-depth foundation area, usually located under a structure's first floor.

Downspout: the metal pipe used to drain water from a roof.

Drainage grade: a surface slope for water runoff.

Eave: the portion of a building overhanging a wall.

Flashings: sheet metal used for waterproofing.

Foundation: an underlying support base of a home.

GFCI (ground fault circuit interrupter): a breaker that shuts off electricity when it senses problems in the circuit.

Grade: a sloping surface.

Hollow-core door: a door made from various woods and wood derivatives that contains interspersed hollow spaces.

Home inspection: the examination of structural components of a building or home by an inspector.

Humidity: air dampness caused by water vapor.

HVAC: heating, ventilation, and air conditioning.

Inspector: a person employed to view and scrutinize structural items.

Insulation: a material that can be placed in parts of a building that will significantly diminish the heat flow rate.

Moisture meter: instrument used to detect dampness.

Narrative report: a lengthy and detailed report describing what a home inspector checked and discovered during an inspection.

Radon: a radioactive gas that can leak into a home from the ground.

Slab-on grade: a type of construction in which a concrete slab serves as both the foundation and floor surface.

Soffit: the underside of a structural overhang.

Index

A

Accountant, hiring a, 23
Additional services, offering, 3, 13, 57, 61, 77–78
Agreements, pre-inspection, 41–43
American Home Inspectors Training Institute, 13
American Society of Home Inspectors (ASHI), ashi.org, membership in, 76–77, 104–105, 107
Answering service, 95
Appendix, home inspection resources, 107–111
Appliances, 67
Associations, industry, 23, 76–77, 104–105
    list of, 107–108
Attics, 55
Attorney, hiring a, 23, 38–40

B

Backgrounds of home inspectors, 5–7
Bathrooms, 54
Billing, 61
Bookkeeping, 96, 98
Books, recommended, 108
Business plan, 16–17
    pre-business checklist, 8
Business structure, 36–37
Buying an existing business, 15

C

Certification, 75–76, 79
Checklist report, pre-printed, 58–59
Chimney inspection, 67
Climate considerations, 52
Code compliance, 53
"Code of Ethics," *American Society of Home Inspectors (ASHI), ashi.org*, 4, 43
Communication skills, importance of both verbal and written, 9–10, 38–40, 102–103
Competition, researching your, 12–13

Computer equipment, 25–27
Consistency, 104
Contracts, 41–43
    list of elements to include in a home
        inspection, 42–43
Conventions and expos, 108
Cross-promotion, 84
Cross-training, 79
Curiosity, natural, 10
Customer
    base, 4–5
    prospective, 12–13, 102–103
    service, 90, 105

D

Decking and porch areas, 63
Delivery of home inspection report, 60
Demographic research, 12–15
Detective, home inspector as, 46–47
Direct mail advertising, 85
Doors, windows and trim, 53, 67
Downturns, surviving market, 7–8

E

E-mail newsletter, 85
Electrical inspection, 51, 52–53, 54, 65
Employees, 94–96
    outsourcing options, 95–96
    payroll and taxes, 94–95
Environmental services, 77
Equipment, 24–29
    basics, worksheet, 30–31
Ethics and standards, 43
Experience in construction, engineering or
    remodeling as necessity in home
    inspection trade, 103
Expert witness services, 77–78
Experts, home inspection, 108–109
Exterior exam, 50–51

F

Failure, common reasons for, 102
Fees, collecting, 61

Financial statements, 98–99
Finishing touches, 56
Flexibility as attribute in home inspection
    field, 7–8
Flier distribution, 5
Follow-up and consultation services,
    60–61, 79
Forms, 109
Foundation and structure of home, 50, 51,
    64
Foundation of Real Estate Appraisers (FREA),
    40–41
Franchises, 109
    vs. independent business owner, 15–16
Fundamentals, inspection, 47
Funding your start-up, 99–100

G

Garage inspection, 53, 64
Generalist, ability to function as a, 8–9
"Get it in writing," 41–43
Glossary, 113–114
Government agencies, 109
Growth of home inspection field, 2–4

H

Health and safety issues, addressing, 57
Heating and cooling, 50, 56, 66
Helpful hints for inspection day, 52
Hidden defects, finding, 46–47
Home inspection report, 58–61
    as marketing tool, 83–84
Home inspection, tagging along on a,
    49–57
Home study/correspondence courses, 110
Homebased business, 18, 20
Honesty, 104
House position and drainage, 63

I

Income and operating expenses, 92–93
Income potential, 2–3, 92
Incorporating, 37

Insider advice, 101–105

Insulation inspection, 64–65

Insurance coverage, 24, 40–41, 79

Interior observations, 66–67

Interpersonal skills, 9–10

K

Kitchens, 54–55

L

Landscaping issues, 51

Lawyer, hiring a, 23, 38–40

Leaky pipes and water spots, 54–55

Legal challenges, 38–40, 103

Liability, 24, 40–41

Licenses and permits, 36

Licensing and certification, 75–76, 79

Location, business, 18, 20

M

Market potential, determining, 12–15

Market research, 11–20

Marketing, 81–90

Marketing consultant, hiring a, 89–90

Mission statement, 17–18
  worksheet, 19

N

Naming your business, 17

Narrative report, home inspector's, 59–61
  sample of, 62–70

*National Association of Home Inspectors
  (NAHI)*, training, licensing and membership in, 77, 108

Networking, 3, 84–85

Newsletter
  as promotional tool, 82
  e-mail, 85
  sample, 83

O

Office equipment, 24, 27–29

Office space, 20, 92

Offshoots of home inspection work, 77–78

Operating expenses, 92–93
  estimating your income and, 97

Opinions, avoid voicing strong, 102–103

Overview of industry, 1–10

P

Partnership, 37–38

Personality traits of successful home
  inspectors, 7–10

Perspective, keeping, 102–103

Phone/cell phone options, 27, 95

Pitfalls, common, 102

Plumbing, 52, 53, 65–66

Pre-sale inspection, 3

Pricing your services, 61

Problems, list of common, 49

Problems, list of common potential,
  56–57

Professional image, creating a, 82–84

Publications, trade, 22–23, 111

R

Radon testing, 57–58
  resources, 110

Realtors
  cultivating relationships with, 4–5
  networking with, 84–85

Record-keeping, 96, 98

Referrals, client, broker, banker and other
  inspectors, 82

Reporting software, 110

Reporting your findings, 58

Resources, home inspection, 107–111

Roofing, 50, 64

S

Selling yourself, 81–90, 102

Service-oriented business, home inspection as, 105

Siding and trim, 50, 63

Sixth sense, 10

Small Business Administration (SBA),
  sba.gov, 8, 103, 109

▲

Software
    accounting/data entry, 26–27
    reporting, 26, 110
Sole proprietorship, 36–37
Special investigations work, 78
Special promotions, 84, 88
Specialized services, offering, 3, 13, 57, 61, 77–78
"Standards of Practice," *American Society of Home Inspectors (ASHI), ashi.org,* 3–4, 43
Start-up capital, 23
Start-up costs, 21–34
Start-up expenses
    for two hypothetical home inspection companies, 32–33
    worksheet, 34
Start-up financing, 99–100
Start-up scenario, 2–3
State licensing exams, 75–76
Stories from the trenches, 47–48
Success
    recipe for, 103–104
    seven tips for, 79
Successful home inspection service owners, 110
Survey, market research, 12, 14
Swimming pool inspections, 48, 51, 52–53

T
"Taking it slowly," 104–105
"Taking the high road," 104
Target market, identifying your, 13
Taxes, 36–37
    and accurate record-keeping, 96
Tools
    home inspection, 25, 27–28
    home inspection suppliers, 111
Trade publications, 22–23, 111
Training programs and schools, 22–23, 72–75, 79, 111

V
Vehicle, company, 22, 83
Voice mail, 95

W
Walkway and driveway, 63
Web site, company, 79, 86–88, 89, 90
Wood stove inspection, 67

Y
Yellow Pages advertising, 5, 82, 88